El Serviazgo A

Iván

i

ii

From My Vision:

Serviazgo is a tangible expression of organizational mystique; it is a differentiator, a success factor, and a competitive advantage.

Serviazgo is about Inspiring and Demanding by raising standards of living, which means transcending from merely transactional relationships to transformational relationships.

Serviazgo, in short, is a philosophy; it is a lifestyle and a model for happiness.

Serviazgo described in one sentence: "To understand that this life is not about Me but about what can happen through Me."

Iván Mancillas

Acknowledgments

> "If I have seen further it is by standing on the shoulders of giants."
>
> Isaac Newton

Throughout the book I express my gratitude to the many people who contributed their inspiring leadership and testimonials. Special thanks, however, go to Compartamos Banco for making this project a reality; to its executives and leadership team for sharing their knowhow with me and helping me make a book that synthesizes the collective knowledge and lessons in leadership accrued over the years. The result, this Comprehensive Servant Leadership Model, contains the ideas, concepts and experiences that have made us successful in our personal as well as professional lives.

Many thanks to all the people and organizations that have collaborated very closely on the leadership programs: Jerrilou Johnson, Miguel Loza, Claudia Mancillas, Unidos Somos Iguales, Javier Santiago, Francisco Arenas, Joel Cryer (R.I.P.), Eduardo Fuentes (of Campo de Retos Krasiba), Cathy Salit, Fernando Trejo (of Deporte 6 am), Rodrigo Jordán and Carlos Sandoval.

This book puts readers in touch with practical, concrete and effective means to achieve a fulfilling life in all the spheres and aspects of development.

Thanks to everyone, as together we've been able to build this model. I'm especially grateful to Carlos Labarthe for the trust he placed in me and for his unconditional support in making this book a reality. I'm also grateful to my good friend Pedro Saucedo, because he was the one who oversaw the book's organization, design, layout and publishing.

I am, of course, thankful time and again to God for giving me the opportunity, the wherewithal and the privilege of being able to serve Him in some way over the years and in the writing and publishing of this book, which I hope will be of use and inspiration to many people.

My deepest gratitude to my loving family, Chriss, Lorenzo, Gonzalo and Marcelo, my great support system. They inspire me and infuse my life with a sense of purpose.

Iván Mancillas

Foreword

"Happy are they who dream big dreams and are willing to pay the price to make them come true." This phrase that was on a picture my brother Pepe had hanging in his room really caught my attention ever since I was a child. Happiness is one of the great mysteries of people's lives. Everybody wants it, and in one way or another we all look for a way to be happy. It's one of those mysterious, built-in "callings". My theory is that God wants us happy because He made us "in His image and likeness" (Genesis 1). He is happy and wants everybody happy. At times, though, finding happiness can be extremely hard. We hunt for it in various ways and in different places: some seek it in material things and life's pleasures; others look for it inside their very soul; still others in carrying out huge projects; others within the family itself, and there are those who think they've found it when they feel someone loves them. Indeed, the search for happiness is one of people's main tasks. I firmly believe that happiness is intimately related with one's own dreams. That's why the opening phrase in this foreword resonates so strongly in me. You and I can gradually become what we dream.

A writer I read years ago even suggests keeping a personal dream journal and writing down our dreams, big and small, to enable us to go over them as we move along in life. Insofar as we realize our dreams, we turn into that person we once dreamed of being.

I have known Iván ever since we were both studying engineering, over 25 years ago, and volunteered in several projects together. A few years later, I asked him to start up a communal bank project, the seed of what is now Compartamos Banco. It is truly a privilege to have been and continue to be with him and with several other people such as Carlos Danel, José Ignacio Ávalos, Miguel Ángel Ortega, Pedro Saucedo and others in putting together such a marvelous project as Compartamos. Words fail me in thanking God for having brought such fabulous people into my life. For me, this has been a road to happiness, to feeling useful, to excelling.

I think Iván's book is a sort of guidebook to happiness. The relevance

3

of the Comprehensive Servant Leadership Model (CSLM) lies in that it is essentially a practical, effective and useful tool for gaining happiness. It is a powerful, efficient model that helps us with our job of making ourselves into better persons, a key to being happy. It is a model that is based on self knowledge, which leads us to turn ourselves into what we ought to be, to become the best version of ourselves, to be *worthy* children of God, to be who He wants us to be, to fulfill our life's mission. We are all born for something, we have a unique, never-to-be-repeated mission in life, and to a great extent finding and fulfilling it is crucial for our full development and happiness.

You and I grow from a base of our major strengths, a kind of launching pad if you will. They are our tools for contributing to embellishing creation, to making it more just, cordial, organized and equal. It's how we help God improve the world; it's how we contribute to the common good. Our strengths, well focused, in line with our personal mission, are not only our own engine of growth, but also the selfsame engine of growth for society. This is why the CSLM can be so useful in our lives.

I can personally attest that using the CSLM and my life plan have been incredibly good and effective for my happiness and fulfillment. Just like Iván says in the book, these elements complement each other in powerful and outstanding ways. Allow me to explain: the CSLM is a tool for growth, and the life plan helps us identify our main shortcoming and enables us to keep it under control and develop our virtues to counter that defect. In other words, the life plan keeps us from getting off track. We all know folks who have gotten off track in their lives, and maybe if they had struggled and worked against their main shortcoming, this would not have happened. I expect that becoming familiar with the CSLM and making a life plan will be useful for you.

Inspirational leaders. Here's an exercise: think about who you consider an inspirational leader, the person or persons who have truly inspired you to become a better person. It can be a well-known, prominent figure or, just as well, someone close to you who has achieved little or no notoriety. Now name the qualities that you have noticed this inspirational leader has. I'm pretty sure that the leader you are thinking of and who has inspired you has somehow gone out of his or her way for others. (S)He is

4

someone who has sought your wellbeing or the wellbeing of society as a whole, someone who has done something good for you or for others, someone who has perhaps made sacrifices, big and small, to make the world a better place in which to live. If we want to be *inspirational leaders*, we must do the same. Let's seek a better world for our children, a more just and fulfilling society, a society with more and better opportunities for all, a society in which people can develop fully. This is why it is so pertinent to have inspirational leaders. They are the ones who build happy, fulfilled families; they take part in projects that change the face of Mexico and the world; they are part of something bigger than themselves, and therein lies, to a large extent, happiness.

Viktor Frankl was a prisoner in a Nazi concentration camp during World War II, and the bulk of his theories about happiness and the meaning of life are grounded in what he lived through in those extermination camps. He states: "Happiness cannot be pursued (... it) is the unintended side effect of one's personal dedication to a cause greater than oneself..."

Therein is the adventure in this book: it asks us to dare to seek happiness, to be inspirational leaders whose leadership is grounded in being of service to others, in *Servant Leadership*. I hope you enjoy it as much as I have and that it becomes a tool for helping you to build the best possible version of yourself.

Carlos Labarthe

Introduction

Leading a full, rewarding life and having a clear sense of purpose are essential to personal fulfillment and reaching the goals we set ourselves, putting us firmly on the path to becoming effective leaders who produce results; inspirational leaders who serve others.

This book is particularly aimed at people who seek such a sense of purpose in their lives and who wish to become inspirational leaders.

It is a necessary book, because more and more people are getting their priorities confused and losing sight of their values for lack of role models, causing them to lose their way in life.

Compartamos began as a volunteer project run by university students to provide support and opportunities for marginalized communities in Mexico. Before long, we were incorporated as a private charity (I.A.P., Spanish initials).

In 2000, Compartamos embarked on a new phase, this time as a limited purpose financial company (SFOL), and by 2006 we had evolved into Banco Compartamos, S.A., a multipurpose banking institution.

Our company continued to grow, and such was our impact that by 2007 we were in a position to make an initial public offering (IPO). Today we are a public company that trades on the Mexican Stock Exchange.

In 2012, Compartamos underwent another metamorphosis, to become a holding for Compartamos Banco, Yastás, Aterna, Fundación Compartamos, Financiera Compartamos in Peru and Compartamos in Guatemala. In 2013, our identity as a group evolved into Gentera.

This is an ambitious book in which we share with readers the lessons we have learned about the nature of inspirational leadership based on our own experiences —lessons that are not likely to be watered down or distorted over time. The challenge was to present this information in a useful, clear and practical way. However, I would like to point out that although this book contains many personal anecdotes, it is not intended to be autobiographical nor does it aspire to document the history of Compartamos.

We have included testimonials and thoughts related to the concept of inspirational leadership and that shed light on its meaning, as well as the knowledge and experiences of many people whom I personally admire and respect —people with whom I have had the pleasure and privilege of working with for more than 20 years. I would like to thank all of them for influence in my journey toward self-realization, personal growth and transformation.

In the first part of the book, I share some personal experiences and specific testimonials on what it means to be an inspirational leader.

In the second part, the reader will find our Comprehensive Servant Leadership Model, a practical and highly effective leadership model and tool based on collective experiences and knowledge that anyone who aims to become an inspirational leader will find useful.

This book would not have been possible were it not for the hard work, dedication and professionalism of the Gentera Leadership Team. Our intention is to share it with as many people as possible in the shortest possible time, and I sincerely hope it reaches all those interested in making the necessary changes, so as to lead a full and rewarding life.

I would especially like to thank all those who have participated in the Gentera Leadership Programs, especially the facilitators, whose input and feedback have provided the raw material underpinning the book's contents.

Servant Leadership

The words "service" and "leadership" come together to define a new way of understanding inspirational leadership. An innovative approach in which self-knowledge and the ability to achieve results lead us not only to realize our dreams but to inspire those around us to chase theirs.

———

The term "Servant Leadership" combines the ideas of "service" and "leadership". Thus, Servant Leadership is leadership based on serving others, serving being understood as brotherly love, charity and solidarity, as preached by Jesus Christ and Saint Teresa of Calcutta.

The first time I heard the term "Servant Leadership" was in 2004, when I met Jerrilou Johnson, who translated it into Spanish as *"Serviazgo"*. Since then, I have identified with the concept and its meaning, and consciously strive to put it into practice.

The Servant Leadership concept was developed by Robert Greenleaf, who states in his book *The Servant as Leader* (1970) that "The great leader is seen as servant first." It is a statement that has sparked controversy. Some feel the concept of Servant Leadership is somewhat weak, while others simply don't feel comfortable with it, since they believe it undermines their credibility, authority or efficacy, or because they are of the opinion that someone who serves can't lead, as the two conflict.

But I pose the question, isn't Jesus –the perfect model of a leader who served, who lived Servant Leadership– the best example of an inspirational leader? Someone who lives and breathes Servant Leadership is destined to become an inspirational leader, and someone who inspires others is necessarily someone who commands respect, who is reliable, respectable, consistent, upright, honest, supportive and generous, someone who lives mysticism, someone who lives according to a set of appropriate values and behaviors, i.e. someone whose path and purpose are commendable.

An inspirational leader is someone who possesses and uses self-knowledge to pinpoint and recognize his/her own motives, values and abilities. These kinds of people are capable of weaving a personal support network through which to give their lives a sense of purpose.

An inspirational leader is someone who serves and shapes others, someone who is constantly growing and who achieves results by virtue of that growth.

them, you become a source of inspiration for others

In other words, an inspirational leader is someone who has a clear idea of where he is headed, who acts with good intentions and who can clearly and objectively differentiate the "whys" and "what fors" for what they are: the "whys" are external and the "what fors" internal.

When they come looking for me, may they find you, Lord

Taking ten minutes to analyze the "what for" and "why" before we launch into any activity or experience can have a marked difference on the final outcome.

> An inspirational leader is someone who serves and shapes others, someone who is constantly growing and who achieves results by virtue of that growth.

People who consistently take the time to ask themselves what for or why they do certain things or engage in certain activities will eventually – and inevitably– find God in their lives.

An inspirational leader knows his own and, like the good shepherd who leads his flock and doesn't ask anything of it he is not willing to do himself, he is never far away and always available. The good shepherd knows his sheep and they know him *(The Gospel according to St. Mark,* 10:14).

> "Soft ways, firm intentions".
> School of Faith

You and I have both the privilege and the huge responsibility of "inspiring others". But more than a great challenge, becoming an inspirational leader requires unfailing commitment.

Only if we are consistent, reliable, upright, responsible, honest and capable can we inspire others. It seems unattainable, doesn't it? Aspiring to be an inspirational leader is a lofty goal that can take a lifetime to achieve. Yet that is our calling: to become the best possible version of ourselves.

Your actions are so loud I can't hear your words

Every day, you and I must aspire to become inspirational leaders, procuring everyone with whom we live and work.

As inspirational leaders, we are responsible for helping those around us realize their dreams. With our support and, more importantly, our example and inspiration, they will no doubt be able to do so, and the achievement will be ours, too, since we shared the responsibility with them.

One of the principles of good inspirational leadership is to know your own. This doesn't just mean knowing the names of those around you, but the names of their family members, understanding their personal challenges, problems, what makes them tick and especially their dreams, since they are the reason we get up every morning.

That said, "You can't give what you don't have," which means that in order to meet our calling to be inspirational leaders, we must first be clear on our own values and motives. We must also have a support network, i.e. a group of people who are always there for us, and be committed to acting with integrity in all spheres of life: family, intellectual, physical and mental health, social, spiritual and professional.

To determine whether someone is implementing Servant Leadership – true leadership based on serving others– suffice to look at how they are addressing the four essential commitments undertaken by every good leader: to serve, form others, grow and produce results. We will examine these four elements in greater detail in the second part of the book.

> An inspirational leader is versed in the art of inspiration but has the wisdom to know when to demand more.

Inspiration is what moves us

Imposing and inspiring are two totally different issues. Inspiration implies conferring meaning. We should remember that conviction inspires and that real-life testimony is the purest source of inspiration.

An inspirational leader is someone who worries about others and is always creating appropriate contexts within which we can realize our full potential.

Often the words power and moral authority are used interchangeably, but there is a major difference between them: power is granted and moral authority is earned. As leaders, it is extremely important we be clear on this point.

For example, power (specifically the power of investiture) is acquired when we are appointed to a certain position, but once we are stripped of that position, we are stripped of the power that comes with it. Power, then,

Moral authority is earned gradually with respect, trust, responsibility and integrity and remains intact regardless of the position or title we hold. As such, it travels from the bottom up, and because it is created from the inside out, it is immune to external factors.

An inspirational leader is versed in the art of inspiration but has the wisdom to know when to demand more. Just as he uses his left hand, so he uses his right.

> "If your actions *inspire* others to dream more,
> learn more, do more and become more, you are a leader.
> *John Quincy Adams, 6ᵗʰ president of the United States*

This short story illustrates different approaches to leadership. Once there was a cook whose teenage daughter came to him overwhelmed with problems. No matter how hard she tried, she said, she couldn't seem to find a solution. He took her into his kitchen and put three pots of water on the stove to boil, all the while listening to her pour her heart out.

The cook then asked his daughter to come over to the stove and watch carefully. She looked on with curiosity as her father took a carrot from a basket and put it in one of the pots. Then he put an egg in the second pot and some coffee in the third. After the water in all three pots was boiling, he told his daughter to fish the carrot out and put it on a plate. He then asked her what the carrot was like before it entered the boiling water and what is was like after. She said that at first it was hard and that after being boiled it had softened.

Then he told her to take the egg out and asked her the same question. She said that the egg was fragile before entering the water, but that it had hardened on the inside when it came out.

Finally, he poured the coffee into a cup and asked her the same question. She replied that the coffee had a distinct aroma and consistency but that it acquired a different flavor after being dissolved in boiling water.

The girl then turned to her father and asked what the meaning of the exercise was. In a show of fatherly love, the cook replied that, just like these three foods, we all face trying situations and adversities. Confronted with the same adversity –boiling water–, all three reacted differently.

> When adversity strikes, we should ask ourselves,
> what am I like today?

when adversity struck it became soft and fragile. Others, like the egg, seem weak, fragile and vulnerable, but when faced with a loss or pain, their hearts harden. The coffee, however, is like the inspirational leader who, when faced with a difficult situation, transforms it, imbuing it with his own aroma and flavor, his own personal stamp, so to speak, that confers it meaning.

When adversity strikes, we should ask ourselves, what am I like today? Like the carrot, the egg or the coffee? How should I tackle the obstacles life throws my way?

When asked to describe an inspirational leader, I immediately picture people who act of their own free will, out of the conviction that their actions are necessary and in the interests of the greater good.

"The concept of 'inspirational leader' is part of the Gentera DNA. It did not come from outside but was created from within, by asking ourselves, "What is Gentera; how do we do things; what do we want to do, and therefore, what is our style?"

Carlos Danel Cendoya, co-founder of Compartamos

"Serviazgo is a process of generating professional and personal tools through which the person's talents are empowered to emphasize their leadership style through self-knowledge, confidence, unity, and human sense. It is a process of personal transformation."

Susana Vidals, regional sales director

"The concept of Servant Leadership has helped me with so many things in the various realms of my life: personal, work and family."

Paulina Murguía Guerrero, corporate strategy

"It's great that we give service, but we must give it a special stamp. We work with the best company, the one that's known for Servant Leadership, for seeking out quality leaders, inspirational leaders who are able to get people to follow them, not through imposition but through inspiration, by being a role model, taking on the major task of role modeling. That is the huge contribution from Servant Leadership: being able to go back and forth

12

inspirational leadership stamp. In the regions I'm in charge of —very different regions up north and down south—, the same seed has taken root, a leadership style that's unique."

Miguel Ángel Ortega Pacheco, regional sales director

"One example of inspirational leadership that left its mark on me was when there was a disaster in Chiapas and I saw Carlos Labarthe arrive where it had happened. Credit flow had been blocked, we couldn't give out money, but Carlos said, 'We've got to get the economy rolling, because nobody is doing it.' We knew this might mean a lot of money down the drain and the possibility of not being able to start back up in the future, but we decided to do it, because it was in the people's best interest. We went out on a limb, and the people went to work. The town spirit picked up, the economy turned around and that changed everything."

Horacio D'argence González, leadership

My Experience with Servant Leadership

Every experience in life is an opportunity to put Servant Leadership into practice. It is our responsibility to create leaders, not followers, and this is achieved every day, in everything we do, with the family, at school, forming work teams and everything we get involved with.
The trick is to achieve a balance between inspiring others and demanding more of them, something that is only possible if we truly commit ourselves to service in action.

———

This chapter contains some personal anecdotes concerning my experience of effective inspirational leadership in action. I would like to share them with you because they have had a huge influence on me and have contributed to my personal transformation.

These experiences and the example I've had of Servant Leadership have all left a deep impression on me. Obviously not all have been of a personal nature; some have come from observing people around me concretely putting Servant Leadership into practice, and their actions have shaped me.

I would like to take this opportunity to thank all the teachers I have had over the years, all the inspirational leaders who have had a positive influence on my life and have served as role models for me.

Before discussing some of the experiences, I would like to tell you a short story, which I think gets my message across. Once upon a time, a hen and a pig lived on a farm. One day the hen turned to the pig and said sardonically: "Tomorrow you're going to die." The pig asked in fear: "What? Did you hear something? How do you know I'm going to die tomorrow?"

The hen replied, "That's right, you're going to die tomorrow because yesterday I was near the kitchen and I heard the cook say, 'Tomorrow we're going to stuff that hen with bacon.'"

In light of the moral of this story, I recommend you pay attention to the messages behind the anecdotes in this chapter, each of which illustrates the skills, qualities and virtues of inspirational leaders, the tools they employ and the conducts required of them.

All these experiences form the backbone of the Comprehensive Servant Leadership Model discussed in this book.

Fourth Grade Elementary School

When I was ten, I went to school at the Colegio La Salle Boulevares, and like any kid my age, I always looked forward to summer vacation. Maybe I was so eager for school to be over that my wish actually came true. That year, my summer began in early May, when I was diagnosed with hepatitis.

I was told I wouldn't be able to attend school for two months, until my treatment ended and I was all better. At first I was overjoyed, thinking, "Now I'll have four months of vacation!" But my happiness was short-lived, when it occurred to me that I might have to repeat the year.

My mother went to notify the school, and the next day, the doorbell rang. Much to my surprise and good fortune, there was my fourth-grade teacher, Rafael Fuentes, who had come to visit me. He offered to come every day after class and bring me the notes and homework so I could finish the year. He didn't worry about the risk of catching hepatitis.

When I close my eyes and remember Mr. Fuentes, I can still see his bright eyes and big smile. I particularly remember his generosity and natural service orientation.

15

To this day, he remains in my heart because of the kind way he made me feel so special and valued. I only hope I thanked him accordingly.

It's been 33 years, and when I think back, I have to admit I'm impressed at how an experience I had at age ten continues to leave its mark on me. What was indubitably one of my first encounters with Servant Leadership makes me aware of the huge responsibility we have as inspirational leaders, a responsibility Mr. Fuentes assumed when he led by example and shaped me forever with his generosity.

> In life, you should never lose sight of your roots or your route.
>
> *José Luis Olivares[1]*

The Seeds of Tae Kwon Do

When I was 11, my mother took me to my first Tae Kwon Do class. The school was right next to the Torres de Satélite, and my instructor was Héctor Olivares, who was known for his way with children. He was the one who sowed those initial seeds of respect, discipline and passion in me. His influence on my life was so strong that when I had children of my own, many years later, I sent them to take classes with him.

As a teenager, I started training with Héctor's brother, José Luis Olivares. From day one, he became my role model, teaching me self-confidence, trust, respect and integrity. To a large extent, it was the

---

[1] Professor José Luis Olivares, the first Mexican to achieve an 8th degree black belt in Tae Kwon Do, has been a teacher of the sport for 43 of his 44 years of practice. Founder and president of the Mexican Institute of Taekwondo since 1980.

perseverance Tae Kwon Do requires that forced me to grow and shaped me as a person.

At that point in my young life I had lots of dreams and the chance to try my hand at all kinds of activities, so I lacked the persistence Tae Kwon Do demands. Nonetheless, I went back again and again, always encountering the same example of self-confidence, respect, trust and integrity. "Nothing beats perseverance," José Luis would drum into us during training.

José Luis Olivares was a major influence on me, and I owe my leadership skills to his example. He has given classes, uninterruptedly, for over 43 years. Demanding and firm, but caring and motivated, it is largely thanks to his dedication that the Mexican Tae Kwon Do Institute has won 35 medals at world championships and the Pan-American Games. In the words of José Luis: "I believed it possible, and that's what I conveyed." Life, I remember him saying, can be summed up in one word: attitude. Ten percent is what happens to you and the other 90 percent is how you react to it.

In each class he would pass on his knowledge and always had a word of encouragement or would say something to get his students thinking and developing. Some of his motivational phrases were: "When the flesh flags, the spirit takes over" and "In life, you should never lose sight of your roots or your route."

Every time I train, I recall what he taught me and am grateful for the opportunity to have had him as an instructor. His words still echo in my head, and Tae Kwon Do has been one of the cornerstones of my personal growth.

Something else I am grateful to José Luis and Héctor Olivares for is the example they set me as brothers. Their exemplary relationship has inspired me to treat those around me as impeccably and with as much respect as they always treated each other.

Models of consistency and integrity –qualities essential to the inspirational leader–, I would like to thank them both for their testimony on life and unimpeachable legacy.

My Fourth School

Academic and discipline problems led me to repeat eighth grade. It was with a sense of failure and frustration that I was forced to move to a new school and leave behind friends, as well as give up privileges at home… Plus, my new school was the fourth I had been in within a very short time. It was all very hard on me. Little did I know there would be more schools to come!

I turned up for my first day at Colegio Durango in my uniform –a burgundy jacket– and was taken aback to find that there was just one classroom for each grade and a small central yard for recess. I was immediately told to get a haircut and go to my classroom. My classmates were other students who were in the same boat as I and were repeating the year, which meant we were all older than the average eighth-grader.

I clicked with three of them off the bat: Abraham, Demetrio and Gaby, an angel who helped me study and do my homework right, who listened to me rant and rave and whose contagious laugh and good mood helped me manage to find peace.

After talking to the threesome, I realized things could be worse and that I might even be able to help them, because they were in an even worse situation than mine.

These were the thoughts that were going through my head when I heard someone yell, "Miss Lucy, the principal, is here!" We all ran to our desks and had no sooner sat down than a woman entered the room. We sat still, afraid to speak. Miss Lucy introduced herself and then called out my name. She asked me to come with her to her office. "I've only been here a day. I haven't done anything yet," I thought to myself.

Lucy Rivera de Sánchez interviewed me in her office and gave me some psychometric tests. For some reason, she wanted to know more about me and help me. From that day on, I felt a connection with her.

I get the impression that my teacher, Mr. Carlos Sánchez, Miss Lucy's son, was in on his mother's plan of action for me. I was frustrated, angry, sad and rebellious, but three surprising events changed all that.

The first one happened on a Wednesday morning. Mr. Sánchez entered the classroom with three ninth-grade students. He picked another three students from our classroom, including myself, and all six of us followed him to the end of the yard, where there was a brick wall. "We've just bought the land behind the school, and we're going to expand the yard. You've been picked to demolish the wall. You have five days," he said, "in which time you won't attend class and won't have any homework. You'll get a free sandwich and soda every day. Here are your mallets. Get to work!"

> "No one can develop for you.
> No one can learn for you. No one
> can grow for you.
> Those are your responsibilities,
> no go-betweens allowed".
>
> *Jorge Bucay*

At that moment, I felt an enormous sense of release and a surge of energy like I hadn't felt in months. I had been given permission to destroy the school, to vent the anger and frustration that had been building up inside me. Needless to say, I was the first to lift the mallet. I hit the wall with all the force I could muster until I had made a hole in it. We all screamed with indescribable joy, and immediately everyone else followed my lead. It didn't take us five days to demolish the wall. By the third day we had razed it to the ground and sat around munching our sandwiches and drinking our free sodas. My friends Abraham and Demetrio were just as happy and free as I was.

> "The function of leadership is to produce more leaders, not more followers."
>
> *Ralph Nader*

The next week I felt like I belonged at school. We hadn't just destroyed something, we had built something, too. I felt the yard was mine because I had helped improve it, and I remember thinking: "Now we'll even look after it." Right away my attitude changed.

The second event, which was totally incredible to me, came about at the end of that same month. Incredibly, I was picked for the honor guard! I got to proudly carry the flag at the following Monday's ceremony.

I now felt useful and appreciated. All that energy and pent-up frustration had found a positive outlet.

Shortly afterwards, the third event occurred. I was invited to play on the school's newly formed basketball team. We practiced every week at a nearby park, because our school had no court. To my surprise, I was named team captain, which was an enormous boost to my self-esteem. We played in several tournaments, winning more often than we lost.

By halfway through the school year, I had come to terms with my situation and adopted a positive, proactive attitude. The fact that Miss Lucy and Mr. Sánchez believed in me meant the world to me, and I thank them from the bottom of my heart for empowering me and constructively channeling my energies and potential. Thanks to their leadership, I was able to enter the next school year and graduate from Colegio Durango with my head held high.

My First Books

I remember one afternoon in October 1984. The doorbell rang, and I peered out an upstairs window to see who it was. It was raining hard, yet I could make out a silhouette, and shortly afterwards, I saw my mother go outside with an umbrella and show the person in. Once I got near the stairs, I instantly recognized his voice. I couldn't believe my mother had even let him past the door! Not only that, but he was in my living room drinking coffee and chatting to my mother as if he knew her. It was a young guy from the neighborhood with whom I had had several run-ins.

To my surprise, he was selling books door to door. I assumed we wouldn't buy anything from him, but my mother thought differently and there was nothing I could do about it. We bought a box of books. A whole box of books!

After he left, I got into an argument with my mother, but instead of apologizing she said: "You should learn from that boy. He's working and making an effort to earn some money, despite the rain. And he seemed very nice to me."

I stood stock-still, thinking "How could something like this happen to me? Something's not right here. There's something I'm not seeing or understanding. It's not fair."

My next reaction was to open the box of books to show my mother the terrible mistake she'd made, but as I took them out of the box one by one, I couldn't help but feel curious. They were all self-help books with titles like *How to Win Friends and Influence People, How to Choose Your People, The Real You, The Magic of Thinking Big, Making Contact, The Greatest Salesman in the World, The Greatest Success in the World, The Christ Commission...*

I devoured them all in a matter of months. I even re-read some of them. They all had a common denominator: simple language and lots of stories. Each one made a lasting impression on me, and I was hungry to learn more about useful subjects for life. Reading them was definitely life altering for a 16-year-old!

Today I am grateful to that "very nice" guy who brought those books to my house and to my mother for teaching me such a valuable lesson that would turn out to be so central in my life. To this day, I am an avid reader of self-help books.

The experience taught me that God acts in mysterious ways and that only to the extent that we are humble and willing to listen and learn from others, especially people we find hard to accept, can we grow and broaden our horizons.

Scouts 186

In 1986, I met my first Boy Scout, and the words that sprang to mind were dedication, motivation, preparation, generosity and enthusiasm. These were qualities incarnated by Héctor Mestre, who invited me to join Troop 186.

But even though these qualities were very clear to me, I was skeptical and joined cautiously. Unfortunately, the Scouts' image had been sullied, and even back then there was a lot of prejudice, which I confess to having shared.

Yet my experience was nothing like the rumors spread by people who have no first-hand knowledge of the organization.

Watching Héctor Mestre and Ladislao de Hoyos lead Troop 186 completely changed my perception.

We climbed the Iztaccíhuatl and Popocatépetl volcanoes several times, went white-water rafting in Amacuzac, played in basketball tournaments (Rover Scout Basketball) and won four years in a row. All these fun activities and other similar challenges taught me to appreciate the importance of working as a team.

In my case, these Scouting activities were a great way to channel my energy positively. I made some good friends, matured and more importantly, developed a sense of belonging.

What struck me most was the generous dedication with which Héctor Mestre organized each activity. He was always the first to arrive and would have everything prepared for us. He would motivate us with jokes and words of encouragement, imbuing the group with his passion and commitment to the Scouts.

This is undeniably a characteristic of an inspirational leader, and I am grateful to Héctor and Scout Troop 186 for the positive influence they had on my life.

Scaling the peaks of Iztaccíhuatl and Popocatépetl at age 18 opened up a whole new world to me, not to mention the opportunity to form bonds of friendship that only people who have climbed a mountain together are familiar with. It was a valuable lesson in teamwork that has been useful in leading teams of my own. The phrase that comes to mind is: "Love isn't what we feel for others, but what we do for them."

Redskins

"Treat people the way they are, and they will get worse. Treat them the way they should be, and they will improve." When I was 18, I'd spend the entire week looking forward to the weekend, when there would invariably be a party or some other plan or challenge.

At the time, I played with the Lomas Verdes Redskins during football season. I was number 89 and played tightend receiver in the intermediate category. I remember we had a particularly hard week of intense training and strategy to prepare for an important game scheduled for the following Sunday.

> Treat people the way they are,
> and they will get worse.
> Treat them the way they should be,
> and they will improve.

We'd trained to perfection and felt ready and motivated to give our best. There was just one hitch: a mega-party had been organized for that Saturday night. We all planned on going and decided to keep it a secret from our coach, Jaime Labastida. Everything was going fine until Jaime came over to some of us at the end of practice on Saturday morning and said in his characteristically firm, no-nonsense tone: "I want you to get to bed early tonight". He may have known about the party or maybe he just knew us so well.

That night before I left for the party, I gave my mother precise instructions: "If the coach calls, tell him I'm asleep. He wants us to train more and asks way too much of us."

The party was incredible, and we were having a ball dancing, singing and doing everything you do at parties, when suddenly the door opened at 11:30. We turned and froze on the spot as our coach

Jaime walked in towards us. The smiles were instantly wiped off our faces. He didn't have to say a word. One look was enough. We knew what we had to do: go straight home.

Early the next day, before the game, he gave us a pep talk, which was harsh but very inspiring. We went out on the field to win, and we did, but Jaime didn't care. Afterwards, he made us run and run and run as punishment for going to the party. That was a more valuable lesson than winning, for sure.

I am grateful to coach Jaime Labastida, R.I.P., for setting an example for me. An inspirational leader, he taught me to demand more of myself and never to throw in the towel. He also taught me the true meaning of the word discipline. Thanks to him, I came to understand the importance of the fine balance between inspiring and demanding.

As a coach, Jaime was always there for his players. He always looked out for us, and just as he left his mark on me, so, I am sure, he influenced every player on the team, which is invaluable for a teenager, a time in life when role models are particularly important.

Gente Nueva[2] 88

They say: "Exemplarity doesn't just shine through in what we do and why, but in how and the ways we use to do it." It's easy to connect

---

2 Gente Nueva: was a social action organization committed to creating a positive-values movement aimed at bolstering personal integrity. It started in 1982, as an initiative by Saint Teresa of Calcutta who, on a visit to Mexico, proposed that a youth group found an organization focused on promoting values. Cultural strengthening, impacting the communications media and social action were the fields tapped to fulfill its mission.

the dots and trace your way back, which is why, in retrospect, I'm grateful to my eighth-grade math teacher at the Instituto Juventud. It was mainly because of her that I failed the year and got expelled. At the time it was a bitter pill to swallow, but if it hadn't been for her, I wouldn't have started university at the same time as Carlos Labarthe, who, in turn, took me to the Gente Nueva group and introduced me to José Ignacio Ávalos.

I was impressed by the way they treated me and the trust they placed in me from day one. It was 1988, and I was invited to act as a host at the I Gente Nueva Congress in Guadalajara. Carlos Labarthe and I were assigned canteen duty for all 8,000 participants.

> Exemplarity doesn't just shine through in what we do and why but in how and the ways we use to do it.

It was an enormous challenge for two 20-year-olds and, once again, I had the chance to find out what it feels like to be trusted, what freedom is and the meaning of service. Not only was it an automatic boost to my self-esteem, but it gave me a sense of responsibility. "I appropriated the task", so to speak, and for the duration of the congress, I had a profound service experience, felt useful and was very happy.

> "Serving is the privilege of kings."

Giving people responsibilities and freedom to act is a wonderful way of showing them you trust them and helping them grow.

26

Furthermore, the conferences and talks I was able to catch at the congress forced me to question the direction my life was taking and many of the activities I was involved in at the time.

I would especially like to thank Carlos Labarthe and José Ignacio Ávalos for leading by example and teaching me the real meaning of service in action. They showed me that, "Serving is the privilege of kings."

The trust and responsibilities they gave me boosted my self-confidence and encouraged me to be more creative.

Father Peter

I was sitting at the back of a small auditorium listening to a "training" talk I'd been invited to when suddenly someone touched my shoulder and said, "Ivan The Terrible" in a broad Irish accent. That was how I met Father Peter Byrne.

Up until then I'd never had the chance to spend time with and get to know a priest. The time had come!

Father Peter made every word count. Every thought, every minute was devoted to instructing me in faith, and he did it with his own unique brand of humor. He invited me to put myself in God's hands, showed me how to draw up a life plan and offered me some practical methods of growing spiritually. But above all, he taught me that following God isn't a question of understanding but rather one of loving.

I am eternally grateful to him for the example he set me. The way he lived his faith and put his trust in God, his optimism and sunny disposition all inspired me to want to grow and be a better person. It is thanks to him that I have a personal relationship with God today.

Father Peter acted as the hand of God, ensuring I was touched by the Lord in my youth. It is because of him that I came to understand we are only as grand as the things we love.

> "Following God isn't a question of understanding but rather one of loving".

The Mancillas Family

I largely attribute my success to having a stable, loving family. Were it not for their support and unconditional love, I would not have had the courage to take risks, much less dare to break the mold, modify my belief system and chase my dreams.

At 21, I decided it was time to make some decisions, decisions that would affect the rest of my life, even though I could only but intuit that back then. Knowing I had a fail-proof support system gave me the confidence and peace of mind to live life to the fullest and develop as a leader.

I recall seeing a TV commercial around that time, announcing the return of a show called *The Pioneers*. It was advertised as a fictional program, when in reality its goal was to drive home the importance of family values. Perhaps they advertised it like that because some people find it hard to believe it is possible to raise a family with values and love, in accordance with God's rules.

I see family as an organization, the domestic equivalent of the Church, the bedrock of society and a school that teaches values.

San Salvador

In October 1992, I traveled to San Salvador, in Central America, to visit Finca International, an organization founded and run by the charismatic John Hatch, whose exemplary way of treating others was a lesson in service.

> "You may not be able to lengthen your life, but you can broaden it".

During that trip, I had the opportunity to see first-hand how the Village Banking system works. These communal banks extend micro-loans to groups of low-income women in remote parts of the country, and it was amazing to see how all these women needed was a helping hand to climb out of the poverty trap and give free rein to their entrepreneurial spirit.

I also got the chance to meet and exchange opinions and experiences with different people, but what struck me most was that, aside from their human leadership skills, all the people I talked to had something in common: they were all dreamers with lofty ideals and an unwavering commitment to helping others.

And when I say commitment, I mean commitment. Just to be clear, let me give you an analogy: commitment is like a plate of ham and eggs. You need two basic ingredients to make it: ham and eggs. And to get these ingredients you need a chicken and a pig. The chicken "participates" with the egg and the pig... the pig sacrifices his own life.

This is the glaring difference between participating and committing to a cause. In life and everything we do, it's up to each of us to decide how we want to live, if we merely want to participate or if we're willing to commit to the point of sacrificing our own lives. We might not be able to lengthen our lives, but we can broaden them.

One day, Carl Shelton visited Compartamos I.A.P. and mentioned he had read about a successful micro-loans project in Bangladesh. The first thing I did was locate Bangladesh on the map, and to my surprise it was right next to Calcutta, where Saint Teresa[3] lived.

In February 1993, I received a copy of *Selecciones*, the Mexican version of *Reader's Digest* magazine, and on page 65 came across an article about the micro-loans project in Bangladesh that Shelton had told us about. "Someone's been copying our idea," I said to myself and started doing some digging. At this point I should remind our younger readers that we didn't have Internet, e-mail or cell phones back then. The only relatively fast means of communicating was by fax. Plus there is a 12-hour time difference between Bangladesh and Mexico, and the language barrier posed another interesting obstacle.

After several months, we were able to make contact and organize a training visit for that July. The next challenge was how we were going to finance the trip. At the time, Compartamos I.A.P. survived solely on donations from individuals and organizations who believed in us and who generously contributed to our cause.

Finally, the big day arrived, a day that was to change our lives forever. Thanks to the support and generosity of José Ignacio Ávalos and Carlos Labarthe, my good friend Pedro Saucedo and I were able to travel to Bangladesh.

The time we spent in rural communities in Bangladesh opened my eyes and taught me a new appreciation for the important things in life. I also learned things I didn't know about myself, like that I could go for days without showering, that I could survive on one meal a day

---

[3] Founder of the religious order of the Missionaries of Charity, established in 1950 in Calcutta, India, to help the poorest of the poor.

for weeks and that I was capable of walking, walking, walking, as well as riding a bicycle through swamps and inhospitable territory for hours on end beneath the pouring rain.

I learned that I had the flexibility to adapt to any situation. I also learned to detach myself from material things but without forgetting my roots or hiding the fact that I was proud to be Mexican.

> "It's nice to be important, but it's more important to be nice."
>
> Seneca

Calcutta, July 28, 1993

On our way back to Mexico we made a stopover in Calcutta, India. We arrived with the mentality that "nothing's impossible" –the same mindset that has characterized the Compartamos team from the outset– and what we wanted was to meet Saint Teresa of Calcutta!

After three failed attempts, our perseverance finally paid off. It was a very special day for me: July 28, my birthday no less. And what better birthday present than to attend a mass with Saint Teresa of Calcutta, receive communion from her hands and be able to exchange a few words with her in person afterwards.

"Small Things with Great Love"[4]

After mass, we told Saint Teresa that she had sowed a seed in us when she visited Acapulco, Mexico, in 1982, to attend a congress on

---

[4] Saint Teresa of Calcutta.

31

family. That seed, we told her, had grown into a tree that was beginning to bear fruit. She gave Pedro and me some medallions and a prayer. We were already attending to over 300 women, and as we talked to her about our plans to reach millions more, she looked me straight in the eye with the sweetest, yet most penetrating gaze I've ever seen and said: "It's not enough, it's not enough."

Pedro and I fell silent and simply asked for her blessing. At that moment, I understood God was telling me loud and clear that serving others is a lifetime mission that entails dedication, commitment and responsibility, that: "Through this inspired woman, God was inviting us to be his helpers."

After that, our vision and mission to serve "revolved around the individual".

The experience reaffirmed my calling and sharpened my sense of purpose. In Bangladesh, I knew that on my return to Mexico we had to do something really big, something that would have a positive, constructive impact on millions of people in our own country.

After San Salvador came Bangladesh, and thank God we were open-minded and humble enough to learn from the two trips.

It seemed we were now clear about our vision and mission and had some ideas as to how to get started. To help us on our way, we had our unwavering faith and a methodology tailored to the people and communities of Mexico.

> "If what you did yesterday seems big, you haven't done anything today."
>
> Lou Holtz

Compartamos, Mexico, 1993

Back in our office, which was in a house on Reforma Lomas 1110 –in the "greenhouse" in the garden, to be more exact, and later in the "tower", a room on the roof that I recall fondly because it was where we came up with many of our plans and spent hours dreaming–, we realized the challenge went by more than one name: explore, undertake, connect, initiate, build, shape...

I am convinced it was no coincidence that the people God chose to be there at that precise moment had no prior experience or paradigms on the subject of moneylending, so we gave free rein to innovation, dreams and action. We may not have had controls, processes, procedures and other such mechanisms in place, but we had a clear sense of purpose and a dream to materialize.

Unlike most projects, organizations and companies, we started out with a powerful motive: the dream of changing our country by offering development opportunities to those most in need of them.

We didn't start out projecting profitability and earnings as a means, core and an end, but as things that would happen along the way. We were fully focused on the mission, the dream, the "what for", and I believe this is the major difference between projects and plans that fail and those that succeed: a dream isn't a goal and shouldn't be planned or viewed as such.

If I dream of the things I already have, the person I already am and my current capacities, my dream will be very limited. After defining a dream, the immediate temptation is to look for ways of overcoming the "hows" and this is where we start to limit ourselves. We begin to clip the wings of our dream and reduce it to a mere a goal.

A dream should be something worth living for, a reason so powerful it is capable of inspiring us and others to chase it and sacrifice our lives for it. It's true what they say about big dreams not needing big wings; all they need is landing gear. As Saint Augustine once said, "It is solved by walking."

Even after volunteering for several years at Gente Nueva and a year working full time at Compartamos, we still weren't clear on the "hows", but we *did* know that we wanted to earn a name for ourselves by doing something for others. We also sought to strike a balance between our personal and professional lives, all the while unaware that we were building an organization that was to be voted among the best places to work in Mexico.

> "Big dreams don't need big wings;
>
> all they need is landing gear".

The Patron Saint of Lost Causes

Almost every day on my way to Compartamos to work, I'd pass Santa Teresita Church. One day I went inside and to my right, a statue of a woman caught my eye. Despite the wound on her forehead, her expression conveyed peace and at her feet was a plaque that read: "Patron Saint of Lost Causes". From that day on, every time I was faced with a challenge that seemed impossible, St. Rita of Cascia[5], as her name was, immediately came to mind. I began to entrust certain problems to her, and, one by one, she found solutions to them. This is how she came to be the patron saint of our dream. When I learned the story of this saint, I was impressed and began to pray more to her.

Faith has been central to this journey. The hand of God and the

---

[5] Santa Rita of Cascia (Roccaporena, Italy 1381 - Cascia, Italy 1457) is considered patron saint of impossible causes and problems.

presence of the Virgin Mary have always been there to guide us.

As the saying goes: "He who doesn't know God could kneel before anyone." From the outset, the challenge for me and for my team has been to stay true to our faith, not just when times are hard but during periods of growth and change. Fortunately, we have managed to preserve our spirituality.

> "Even if a man had everything else: wealth, fame, virtue and so on, he still could not lead a happy life without friends."
>
> Aristotle

Boulder, Colorado, 1995

Continuing to pursue adventure, innovation, and learning, in the summer of 1995, Carlos Labarthe and I decided to take another step toward realizing our dream, by enrolling in a micro-finance course organized by Bob Christen. It was the first course of its kind, and Bob was leading the group of experts who would be sharing their knowledge and experience with 19 green students.

In what you might say was my formal introduction to microfinances, I discovered a whole new world, a whole new industry just waiting to be explored. The bonds of friendship Carlos and I formed with our teachers were to be of enormous help in the evolution of Compartamos, particularly our relationship with Richard Rosenberg[6], who promoted a joint project between the World Bank's

---

[6] Richard Rosenberg is a consultant with the Consultative Group to Assist the Poor (CGAP) and has contributed articles to many of the group's publications. A Harvard Law School graduate, he specializes in matters such as interest rates, excessive debt and microfinance and is a

CGAP[7] partnership and Compartamos.

In Bob Christen[8] and Rich Rosenberg we found not only intellectual leaders, but a couple of good friends and mentors who knew how to bring out the best in us by setting the bar increasingly higher.

The experience helped us develop processes and mechanisms, build trust, and create the transparency required to move forward toward our goal of reaching the greatest number of people in the shortest possible time.

---

leading faculty member for the Boulder Institute Microfinance Training Programs. Before coming to CGAP, Rosenberg was deputy director for the United States Agency for International Development's Center for Economic Growth, where for nine years he oversaw investment promotion, privatization and pension reform programs, as well as financial development activity, in Latin America. www.cgap.org

[7] The Consultative Group to Assist the Poor is an independent policy and research center dedicated to providing access to financing for economically disadvantaged people. It has the support of 30 development agencies and private foundations whose mission in common is to alleviate poverty. Headquartered in the World Bank, CGAP makes available market intelligence, promotes standards, develops innovative solutions and offers consulting to governments, financial service providers, donors and investors. www.cgap.org

[8] Christen is the president and a founding member of the Boulder Institute of Microfinance. He has worked in over 40 countries as a consultant to governments, banks and microfinance service providers. He has also served as director of financial services for the poor at the Bill and Melinda Gates Foundation and as a senior consultant for CGAP at the World Bank. www.bouldermicrofinance.org

I Choose You, and There Is No Going Back. My Time Has Come.

I thought 1993 had been a life-altering year because I'd graduated from university, met Saint Teresa of Calcutta, been to Bangladesh and earned my black belt in Tae Kwon Do. But it was 1995 that was to be the real landmark in my life, the year when I took my wedding vows and put myself in God's hands, accepting the commitment.

In my view, there's only one way of understanding marriage and that's based on faith. Only by trusting God completely can marriage transcend the human plane and blossom into something more than a physical relationship or contract of convenience.

My wife Chrissa filled my life with love and light, changing it forever with her unique personality and creativity. She is my concrete way of loving God, and our family is our concrete way of introducing others to God. I have found self-realization by sharing, having fun together and looking in the same direction.

Marriage has allowed me to grow personally and spiritually, while Chrissa's unconditional love, patience, trust and understanding have encouraged me to develop my skills. She is the person who believes most in me, and that is all I need. One day I gave her a signed copy of my birth certificate as a symbol of my love for her.

She has set me an example with her generosity and dedication. She is and always has been my muse, the nucleus of my support system. I've lost count of the number of times she's had to catch or pick up the towels I've thrown in along the way.

37

God has blessed us with a wonderful family, and our mission in life as a couple and a family is to ensure that we, and all those around us, enter the gates of heaven.

Father Peter Byrne prepared us for marriage and in retrospect, I'm glad he did. With his guidance, we were able to take the same spiritual path as a couple and understand what it meant to put our relationship in God's hands, take it to a higher, not merely human plane, for we were both convinced –and still are– that this is the only way a marriage can work and withstand life's up and downs. At the end of the day, anything is possible when you trust in God.

Santo Domingo, Oaxaca

One experience I enjoyed immensely was visiting rural communities in Oaxaca to meet our clients. Miguel Ángel Ortega, who headed the local team, had gone to a lot of trouble to plan the trip, which would turn out to be one of the most important in Compartamos history.

On that occasion, I had the privilege of meeting Alfredo Harp Helú,[9] a simple man with a grand vision whose help and advice have

---

[9] In 1971, Mexican businessman Alfredo Harp Helú founded and directed the Casa de Bolsa Acciones y Valores (Accival stock brokerage), becoming the CEO of Grupo Financiero Banamex-Accival in 1991. In 2001, Citigroup acquired Grupo Financiero Banamex, and in 2003 he resigned from the Citigroup board of directors. He currently chairs the board of directors of Grupo Financiero Banamex. He has played a major role in developing education in Mexico, never missing the chance to support programs for improving various academic entities. His contributions to Mexico's artistic, cultural and historical patrimony and his commitment to promoting its sports clearly reflect his confidence and involvement in Mexico's transformation. Source: http://2012.los300.com.mx/alfredoharphelu/

been crucial to realizing our dream.

I remember it as if it were yesterday: we arrived with the first group of clients, Crédito Mujer (previously Generadora de Ingresos[10]), and were on schedule for the meeting to begin. The chairwoman of the group got to her feet, and we all stopped talking. She had our full attention. She produced a sheet of paper from her apron and proceeded to unfold it. Then she cleared her throat. There were about 50 people or so waiting for her to give her speech. "Good afternoon to you all and welcome," she said. "First I would like to extend a special welcome to our guest of honor, president and CEO of Banamex, Iván Mancillas."

I was dumbstruck when I heard my name and thought to myself: How could she make a mistake like that? I felt my face and ears burning up and prayed for her to stop talking. I wanted it to be over. I longed for the ground to open and swallow me up. I thought everyone would think I'd written the speech myself. I stared straight ahead without moving an inch, but could hear people muttering and could feel everyone's eyes on me.

Needless to say, no one could talk about anything else during lunch. We all laughed about it later, when I was finally able to relax.

> "Give what you have, that you may deserve what you have not".
>
> Saint Augustine

---

[10] Generators of Income formed a group of 20 to 30 adult women, who received loans to be invested in a productive activity. The group elected a committee (president, secretary and treasurer) to represent them.

That afternoon in Oaxaca, I had a private conversation with Alfredo Harp. We were walking past the Santo Domingo Church, and I took the initiative to ask him for a word of advice. He listened to me attentively and was kind enough to share some ideas and personal experiences that have been extremely useful to me. That was the first of several occasions on which I met with him to discuss a variety of topics.

Alfredo Harp is an inspirational leader whom I respect and admire; a committed man who is generous enough to share his life testimony with everyone around him.

> "The most important thing in communication is hearing what isn't said".
>
> Peter Drucker

Our Clients: Our *Raison d'Être*

This phrase sums up Compartamos' attitude toward its clients, who have set me an example I've never witnessed anywhere else. Their simple, cheerful outlook is a trait common to all those for whom Servant Leadership is part and parcel of their lives.

One of my first conversations with a client was with a woman who told me about everything she and her family hoped to accomplish over the following four months with the 150 pesos Compartamos had loaned her. It should be noted that 150 pesos was the initial amount we lent at that time.

From then on, I was mindful that the more we saved on expenses and the more efficient we were, the more we could lend to our clients at the lowest possible interest rate, thus reaching more and more people who didn't have access to any other type of financing. The principles of responsibility and awareness became more pressing than ever as I attempted to apply and live by them.

That night, back in Mexico City, I went out to a sushi bar for dinner with a couple of friends. Our check came to 450 pesos. I couldn't sleep that night, thinking about my conversation with that woman, and for a while afterwards I suffered from a guilty conscience, until I decided to do something about it and started working on policies, processes and methodologies to further our cause. Naturally, I adjusted and took pertinent measures within my personal life, as well.

New York, 2007

In April 2007, we went to New York to witness Compartamos become a publicly traded company. We were there when its shares appeared on the big board at the New York Stock Exchange.

Compartamos had reached a milestone. We had connected with the markets, and I was overcome with an indescribable mixture of happiness, excitement and satisfaction. We had come this far, but with the accomplishment came an even greater challenge and more responsibility.

As I shared the moment with our incredible team of leaders and friends, I was more convinced than ever that we would be able to fulfill our mission. We were worthy of what God had placed in our path. I knew then he had big plans for us and that we had his blessing to forge ahead with our dream.

Today, when I recall how we started out, our "what for", I thank God for giving us the strength and mindfulness to stand firm and remain true to our faith, which has been vital in executing the Lord's design for us.

I also remember writing a couple of letters back then that took their inspiration from the gospel. Today they remain a constant reminder of my mission and goals. Not only have they helped keep my sights firmly on the path ahead, but they have stopped me from getting distracted by life's fleeting successes and moments of glory. The letter that follows inspired me to reflect on how its teachings could be applied at Compartamos, so I have dared come up with an analogy.

Reading of the first letter from the apostle

Saint Paul to the Corinthians, 13, 1-8

Brothers and sisters, strive for God's greater gifts. And I will show you a still more excellent way. If I speak in the tongues of men or of angels, but do not have love, I am only a resounding gong or a clanging cymbal.

If I have the gift of prophecy and can fathom all mysteries and all knowledge, and if I have a faith that can move mountains, but do not have love, I am nothing.

If I give all I possess to the poor and give over my body to hardship that I may boast, but do not have love, I gain nothing.

Love is patient, love is kind. It does not envy, it does not boast, it is not proud. It does not dishonor others, it is not self-seeking, it is not easily angered, it keeps no record of wrongs. Love does not delight in evil but rejoices with the truth. It always protects, always trusts, always hopes, always perseveres.

Reading of the first letter of Iván Mancillas to Compartamos employees, April 4, 2006

Brothers and sisters, strive for God's greater gifts. And I will show you a still more excellent way. Even if we had the largest corporation in the world with business units in other countries, without faith we are only a resounding bell or a clanging crowd.

Even if we had the most efficient, most comprehensive system, even if we had distribution channels and payment networks the length and breadth of the country, even if we had ten million clients, a highly diversified service and product portfolio and the power to attract all the financing and savings on the market, without faith, we are nothing.

Even if we donated more than two percent of our earnings to charities and social responsibility programs, even if we sacrificed all our family time, without faith it would all be in vain.

Faith is passionate, faith is obliging, faith doesn't work alone; faith is neither irresponsible nor superficial; it does not tire or wane, does not take pleasure in injustice, does not baulk nor bear grudges, but revels in the truth. Faith serves boundlessly, shapes and grows without limits, yields infinite results. Faith transcends and inspires. The work of Compartamos is everlasting.

Kia Kaha

In 2009, my son Lorenzo was studying at the Oaklawn Academy in Wisconsin. One day he called and said, "Dad, I just saw a movie you have to see. I know you're going to like it, and it's going to help you with Compartamos."

I got hold of a copy as soon as I could and was struck by what I saw. Here, in a nutshell, was the definition of inspirational leadership and personal transformation I'd been trying to get across.

43

So, at the following annual Compartamos meetings, we showed *Forever Strong* and held workshops afterwards to discuss its message: *Kia Kaha*[11], which, in the language of the Maoris of New Zealand, is a motivational phrase that was used during World War II and after the devastating earthquake in that country. It means "Everything's going to be all right" and is used to lift others' spirits and inspire them to face adversity with courage. *Kia Kaha* became the motto that underscored our organizational culture, our religion and values. It is an affirmation, a positive statement that works well if you believe in it. And we do.

It can also mean "stay strong", "my thoughts are with you" or "I'm thinking of you". In the Compartamos lexicon, it means stay true to yourself and don't do anything to shame yourself, your family, Compartamos or God. *Kia Kaha:* forever strong!

---

[11] In Maori, one of New Zealand's two official languages, this means to lift the spirits, an affirmation to inspire others to confront adversity with strength. It is a positive statement: "Everything's going to be OK." Another meaning is "Stay strong, I and my thoughts are with you."

Comprehensive Servant Leadership Model (CSLM)

The Comprehensive Servant Leadership Model (CSLM) is a tool Compartamos created that has developed through collective learning. It is designed to teach us to never stop learning, to live each experience fully, to question ourselves and acquire self-knowledge on our journey toward self-realization. A combination of balance, proper motivation, guidance and values leads to a full, rewarding life.

Comprehensive Servant Leadership Model

Background

As a result of Compartamos' steady growth, in mid-2008 we once again encountered the twofold challenge of running an organization while remaining committed to our cause. Except this time we had to do it more urgently and intensely. From day one, we had agreed to put our talent to the service of our faith and had not wandered from this path. So we decided to take a closer look at the strategic aspects of leadership, which, in turn, gave rise to a project we christened "Star-Makers" that was to determine the future of Compartamos.

The Executive Leadership Department was a direct spin-off of the Star-Makers project. It was this department that came up with the Pyxis concept that was to mark the direction of its programs.

In Latin, *pyxis* means "compass", and Pyxis Nautica is a small constellation in the southern sky, so named by Nicolas Louis de Lacaille. We chose the term because the core idea of the project was to create a constellation with a series of "stars" that, together, would shine brighter and encourage the formation of new and even brighter constellations to light the way of other stars, all illuminating the same path and pointing in the same direction.

Executive Leadership Department

The first step to creating this department required some strategic planning that allowed us to define our mission, vision and value proposition, as well as the department's operational profile. The results were as follows:

Mission

To form inspirational leaders based on the acquisition of self-knowledge, and implementation and follow-up of the Comprehensive Servant Leadership Model (CSLM), with the understanding that self-realization will result in maximum levels of social, economic and human value.

Vision

To become experts at radically transforming our co-workers at all Gentera companies by setting them an example of inspirational leadership that sparks, stimulates, enlivens and motivates them in their professional and personal lives.

Value Proposition

To create innovative learning contexts designed to form inspirational leaders.

> "We have co-workers who are convinced of and committed to the efficacy and utility of the Comprehensive Servant Leadership Model, which is based on serving others."
>
> Strategic Statement

Because our co-workers are convinced of and committed to the efficacy and utility of the Comprehensive Servant Leadership Model, which is based on serving others, and are committed to implementing it, we can create innovative learning contexts for the formation of inspirational leaders by identifying specific needs. This enables us to design and implement in-depth personal transformation programs on a permanent and ongoing basis at all the Gentera companies, based on efficient, leading methodologies that equip participants with practical tools to help them serve and lead.

During the strategic planning stage, we got together and decided how the department would be structured and set up the leadership team. To gain experience in areas such as micro-finance and human development that are key to Gentera, we made numerous trips to other countries and specialized organizations. We forged important relationships and took it upon ourselves to learn the latest teaching methodologies. We also worked with expert facilitators, who helped train us so we could train others in areas vital to Gentera by means of certifications, courses, seminars, workshops, readings and film showings.

In keeping with our mission to innovate and to bolster our leadership programs, we have made alliances with certain educational institutions and thus gained greater knowledge on relevant topics. To cite an example, we have benefitted from the advice of and personal contact with several professors at the IPADE business school, in the area of strategic planning. Likewise, we created and strengthened our Content Consultation Committee with teaching and leadership experts who aid us in content design and development. We also participated in the leadership program organized by the *Harvard Business Review* on Easter Island, Chile and visited the Leadership Center for GE executives in Crotonville, New York. Not only are we members of the Association for Experiential Education (AEE), but we have participated in AEE events in Memphis and Las Vegas, visited challenge camps at various universities and experiential education centers in the U.S., such as the University of Charlotte, and received training at the "Lánzate!" leadership center run by the University of Monterrey (UdeM), in northern Mexico. In our drive to implement best practices, we visited the YMCA in New Jersey; learned about the experience of Vertical, a foundation in Chile that specializes in creating leaders; attended the annual Greenleaf Leader as Servant conference in Dallas, and sponsored and participated in the first AEE-Mid-South-Region Conference in Monterrey, Nuevo León, Mexico.

Learning and adopting new approaches involves reading specialized literature. Among the books we consider useful to developing inspirational leadership skills include: *The Servant as a Leader,* by Robert Greenleaf; *Go for Gold,* by John C. Maxwell; *Primal Leadership,* by Daniel Goleman; *True North,* by Bill George; *Blue Ocean Strategy,* by W. Chan Kim; *Humildad y liderazgo,* by Carlos Llano; *Start with Why,* by Simon Sinek; *Smart Talk,* by Lou Tice; *The North Groups,* by Bill George and Doug Baker; *Man's Search for Meaning,* by Viktor Frankl, and *Liderazgo real,* by Rodrigo Jordán, among others listed in our bibliography.

> Learning and adopting new approaches involve reading specialized literature.

In terms of training, we are proud to say our Leadership Department has been certified in the Birkman Method. We have also received training at The Pacific Institute; Performance of a Lifetime in New York; taken the Leadership Diploma Course at the Anáhuac University; trained in high and low-grade challenges at Integra, Camp Krasiba, and we have had an ongoing presence and the benefit of advice from professors at IPADE, where we took part in a 30-month Strategic Planning Review. We have also been certified in first-aid in remote areas; are familiar with the method of the ROI Institute® Iberoamérica in Santiago de Chile[12]; have been certified as professional facilitators by Linkage[13], and participated in the Greenleaf Intensive Servant Leadership Program in Chicago and the Zenger/Folkman Seminar for inspirational leaders.

The Gentera leadership team has over five years of experience. Aside from the professional training we have received, ours is a consolidated team that has acquired the abilities to meet the future needs of Gentera vis-à-vis the creation of inspirational leaders.

From the outset, our programs were designed to foster and consolidate the leadership skills desired by Gentera, which meant we had to define the skills we wanted to develop so we could focus our efforts accordingly.

The first program had three modules in which the activities, sessions and dynamics were aimed specifically at identifying and developing the leadership skills we had already outlined.

As we started implementing the programs, we gradually matured and were able to define our goals more clearly, as well as agree on the "hows" that would get us there, all the while taking pains to ensure that the content, structure and organization of our leadership programs remained true to our vision and mission. We are proud to say that, in time, we have designed and developed our own methodology, which is based on various theories, contents, learning models and methodologies, such as:

---

[12] The institute in Latin America in charge of disseminating, applying and certifying Jack Phillips' Return on Investment model.
[13] A worldwide organizational development firm specializing in developing leaders.

Experiential Education, Challenge by Choice, The Learning Zone (see Figure 1) and a "Learning Model" (see Figure 2).

Figure 1. "Learning Zone"

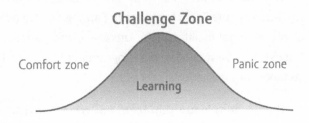

Figure 2. "Learning Model": Learn to Learn

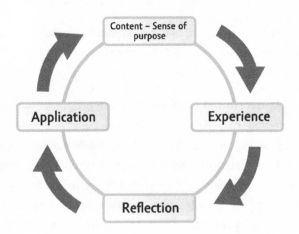

These were the building blocks we started out with and that, with a little trial and error, we were able to adjust so they had a greater impact on our results and on learning and progress indicators.

> The comfort zone is for recovering,
>
> gathering strength and resting up a little,
>
> but not to live in.

We have seen that learning is extremely limited in the comfort zone and that the same goes for the panic zone. In these zones, people are in no condition to learn or experiment, which makes it imperative to push them into the learning zone, using various methodologies and programs. Ideally, we should aim to stay in this zone our entire lives, using the comfort zone only for recovering, gathering strength and resting up a little, but not to live in.

This model begins by suggesting a "what for", which is then reinforced with a content, which could be a case study, a theory, a movie or some other material that stimulates the intellect. Once the "what fors" have been discussed and the case studies analyzed, the concepts and ideas behind them can be assimilated, and it won't be until then that we can move on to the next phase of the "Learning Model", the phase where we live the experience.

A picture says more than a thousand words, but an experience is worth more than a thousand pictures

Only experience can put concepts and theories to the test. Beyond a doubt, the best way of assimilating knowledge is by overcoming a challenge of some kind, be it physical, emotional, intellectual or spiritual. It doesn't matter what the challenge is: "Experience is the best teacher."

51

The next phase of the "Learning Model" is reflection. This is a time when we need to acknowledge our feelings, our emotions, what we've lived, experienced, learned, and connect it all with real life. The hardest and most important part of this phase is to externalize what you are feeling and share it with others.

Reflection is what differentiates a learning experience from a simple experience. Without it, no lessons of value are likely to be learned.

The last phase of the model is its application. During this phase, we apply the knowledge we have acquired and put everything we have reflected on to the test. This will translate into concrete actions that can be implemented and gauged over the next 48 hours.

To the extent that we adopt the Learning Model as part of our lives and use it at every available opportunity, we will become learners –a skill that is essential to the inspirational leader.

In leadership programs, the inspirational leader is assigned a vital role within the organizational chart. This is because he is able to influence the company's vision and operation, depending on the position he occupies within its structure. For example, ideally, the CEO should devote most of his time to developing and working on the company's vision and little to operational concerns, whereas a credit promoter will spend most of his time and effort on operational aspects and very little working on the company's vision.

> To the extent that we adopt the Learning Model as part of our lives and use it at every available opportunity, we will become learners.

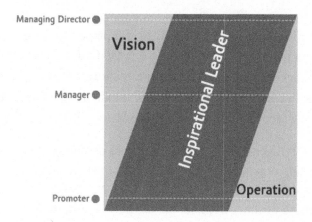

This is not the case, however, when it comes to inspiring others, a quality that is not subject to hierarchy but that remains constant and burns with the same intensity all the time, regardless of corporate structure or position. As such, it is at once a huge challenge and a key factor in success.

After our leadership programs had been in operation for two years, we began asking ourselves what character traits and behaviors had gotten our leaders where they were, individually and as a group. The answer was the sum of their experience accumulated over the years, taking into account the collective conscience and training in inspirational leadership. This is how we gradually built and consolidated the Comprehensive Servant Leadership Model (CSLM).

The CSLM has enabled us to document what it is and has been valuable to us in terms of leadership and faith. It has also allowed us to build on these elements every day, with a view to consolidating the company's future. Today, this model is inseparable from our philosophy and corporate culture.

The challenge is to present it as a life model, in other words, make the intangible tangible, put a name on all the things we have singled out as being meaningful to us and that have brought us success over the years.

When developing the CSLM, we pinpointed one key aspect that lends the model its name: leadership based on serving others. In this context, Servant Leadership transforms the leader into an inspirational leader and both concepts –Servant Leadership and inspirational leadership– are the basis and essence of the model discussed in this book.

It is generally held that the duties and responsibilities of a leader are to plan, organize, coordinate, control, etc., and we accept this without stopping to ask ourselves if it's true. Not only have we been taught to see these qualities as good, but we have appropriated others' paradigms and beliefs about what it takes to be a leader.

The same goes for countless other concepts and beliefs we have either grown up with or adopted just as blindly, concerning faith, marriage, family, health, etc., which is why it is so important to constantly question and reflect on them, to the point where they become qualities and practices intrinsic to our very being and that, as inspirational leaders, we put into practice on a daily basis.

In the case of Gentera, it was especially important to call into question established paradigms and beliefs, because we are an organization that has overturned them when it comes to granting loans. We have no credit committee, demand no guarantees or business analysis and lend money to high-risk customers in rural areas.

When we asked those participating in our leadership programs how a belief or paradigm is formed, we got answers like "They are handed down to us", "By following tradition", "By custom", "Through repetition", "Based on personal experience", all of which are correct. Let's not forget a paradigm can be described as a series of experiences, beliefs and values that affect the way an individual perceives reality and the way he responds to that perception. As such, paradigms help us establish patterns and set limits.

Sometimes we do things without really knowing why we do them. Or we do things a certain way simply because they've "always been done that way" and because it works, we don't question it. But we believe it is important to constantly question old paradigms and build new ones.

> "Between stimulus and response
>
> is the freedom to choose".
>
> Viktor Frankl

It is equally important to understand the difference between reacting and responding, since reacting is completely conditioned by emotions and feelings, whereas the act of responding is linked to reasoning and the intellect. When life throws curveballs at us, we would do well to stop and ask ourselves whether we are reacting or responding. Between stimulus and response is the freedom to choose. We must not forget that we have a pause button, and if we used it more often, we would probably make better choices.

PAUSE BUTTON

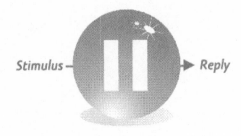

Stimulus → Reply

Between stimulus and response is the freedom to choose.

Victor Frankl

When Change Is Necessary, It's Already Late in Coming

Once there was a seven-year-old boy who liked to draw. One afternoon, he made a drawing and showed it to his big brother, hoping for his approval. Instead, his big brother laughed at him and said: "What's that? It's horrible. I can't even tell what it is!" The boy was upset and went to find his sister, who told him to "Go away, and leave me alone," without as much as looking at him.

I'm sure you can imagine what went through the boy's head. He probably came to the conclusion he had no talent for drawing or worse, that his ideas were worthless and that he wasn't important. To put the icing on the cake, the boy went to his bedroom and stuck the drawing on his wall, but when his father got home, the first thing he did was tear it down and tell his son off for ruining the new paint job, confirming the boy's suspicions that no one loved him.

All it took was one afternoon for the boy to form beliefs and paradigms that were totally out of proportion with his reality. In all likelihood, he never tried drawing again.

Now let's imagine he's an adult. He's at a work meeting with several managers, and his boss asks him to stand up in front of the group and draw something. The odds are he'll enter the panic zone and start hearing a voice in his head telling him over and over again "You can't draw", "They're going to laugh at you", "You're worthless..."

We could probably all cite similar anecdotes that have led us to form beliefs and paradigms that limit us, beliefs and paradigms whose validity we need to question if we are to grow. Perhaps we have been denying ourselves something or holding back because someone or something made us think we weren't worthy of it, and we believed it to the point where we stopped trying. Sometimes the people who have instilled these beliefs in us are the very people we admire and respect, but it's important to remember that even though they may love us and want what's best for us, they may be wrong.

This is where the Comprehensive Servant Leadership Model (CSLM) comes in, because it teaches us, step by step, how our personal belief system was built, what paradigms we live our lives by and which ones hold us back.

That said, paradigms are not intrinsically bad. They are simply patterns or boundaries that are established at a given moment in time to help things run more smoothly, but sometimes they are presented in such a negative way or are so outdated that they stop us and can stunt our development.

This anecdote in a story by Jorge Bucay[14] illustrates my point. One day at the circus, a girl went up to an elephant that was chained to a stake in the ground. The girl asked its tamer why, if it was so big and strong, the elephant didn't pull the stake out of the ground and escape. And the tamer replied: "When the elephant was a baby, it was chained to the stake and

---

[14] Jorge Bucay, "El elefante encadenado", in *Recuentos para Demián*, 27th reprint, Editorial del Nuevo Extremo, Argentina, 2006.

even though it tried to free itself at first, after several days of pulling and tugging it gave up. Today the elephant is big and strong, but he still believes he can't escape, which is why he doesn't even try."

> Paradigms are not intrinsically bad. They are simply patterns or boundaries that are established at a given moment in time to help things run more smoothly.

Bucay's story is an invitation to ask ourselves what chains we've stopped trying to break free from. What are the dreams we gave up on because someone or some circumstance made us think they were impossible? We were convinced or perhaps we even convinced ourselves we weren't deserving or capable of materializing them. But maybe those circumstances have changed. Maybe now is the time to reach for the stars. We need to take the time to revise our beliefs and paradigms, and this is an excellent place to start if we want to develop one of the most important qualities of the inspirational leader: self-knowledge.

Questioning our beliefs and paradigms will eventually bring us to a point where we have to make some life-altering decisions. Perhaps we'll find ourselves forced to take actions that require courage, help, perseverance or willpower, but for change to be lasting it needs to come hand-in-hand with transformation, and when we say transformation, we mean there is no going back.

Just as a caterpillar turns into a butterfly and can't turn back again, so change in ourselves should be based on banishing from our thoughts and actions beliefs and paradigms that no longer apply to us, that are no longer valid and that perhaps weren't even ours to begin with.

Only a deep-rooted, conscious transformation can lead to permanent change. On the subject of transformation, let me remind you of a passage from the Bible[15] where a leper comes up to Jesus and says, "You can cure me if you want" and Jesus said, "I want to" and cures him. Isn't it enough to have faith and say to Jesus, "If you want, you can transform me"? We at Gentera have found the technique developed by Lou Tice (R.I.P.)[16], international speaker and executive president of the Seattle-based Pacific Institute, useful. Tice emphasizes the power of the mind to determine our future success. His technique is based on affirmations, an affirmation being "an emotionally charged statement in the present tense that describes a desired final outcome". In other words, Tice believes an affirmation helps you visualize how you will feel and what emotional state you will live in. Thus, to get what you want, all you have to do is make an affirmation as if you had already obtained it. It's enough to repeat to yourself: "I want, I choose, I decide."

To make the affirmation even more effective, it's important to associate it with images, words and feelings in your mind, to tell yourself, for example: "I live a balanced life and am at peace, because I accept, forgive and devote as much time as necessary to my friends and family"; "I am humble and generous. I serve others with love and devotion"; "I lead a simple, disciplined, focused life, and feel satisfied and fulfilled because the few things I do, I do to the best of my ability and with great mindfulness."

If we repeat these affirmations and believe them, we will become them, because the reality is we're only capable of what we think we're capable of. In other words, we are what we think.

---

[15] Saint Mark 1, 39-45.

[16] Author of *Cultures of Excellence, Personal Coaching for Results, Smart Talk for Achieving Your Potential, Winners Circle Network* and numerous articles. He has worked with NFL teams to develop and raise player potential.

Comprehensive Servant Leadership Model

Comprehensive Servant Leadership Model

Clearly, having children doesn't make you a good parent, just as owning a piano doesn't make you a pianist and being a director doesn't make you a leader. To be good at something, we need tools, and the CSLM is a tool we can use to bring about a deep and lasting transformation in ourselves based on self-knowledge. But before I start describing each of the components of the Comprehensive Servant Leadership Model, it is important to keep in mind, grasp and recall the concept of inspirational leader on which the model is based and experienced. Simply put, the inspirational leader is someone who is enthusiastic, consistent over time, passionate, has a well-defined sense of purpose in life and is aware of his capacities and strengths. He knows which areas of his life he needs to work on, has unwavering values, leads a morally upright life, is familiar with the members of his support system and works to maintain and develop it, is committed to serving and forming others, growing and producing results. He is someone who dreams and encourages others to dream and who constantly seeks to develop the virtues that will help him get there. He is someone who inspires others with his example and who is committed to the greater good.

> Having children doesn't make you a good
> parent, just as owning a piano doesn't make you
> a pianist.

The Comprehensive **Servant Leadership** Model was developed and is used as a tool to transform ourselves into inspirational leaders, something we can achieve by reflecting on, delving into and appropriating each of its components.

> If we work on the components in the CSLM ,
>
> we can move forward safely through a profound
>
> transformation process.

The 11 Components of the CSLM

The Comprehensive Servant Leadership Model has three parts: the internal dimension, the external dimension, and ethics. The internal dimension centers on self-knowledge, i.e. awareness of the six components that guide us internally: abilities, values, motivation and FISSEP (Spanish initials for Family, Intellectual, Mental and Physical Health, Social, Spiritual and Professional aspects), hence its acronym, as well as our support system and sense of purpose.

The external dimension concerns the development of the four visible components that guide us externally or in terms of other people, i.e. serving and forming others, growing and producing results. These four components are the commitments undertaken by the inspirational leader.

And the third part of the model refers to the code of ethics that guides and regulates our internal and external dimensions.

Using the CSLM for meditative purposes helps us gain awareness, develop, and turn all these elements into plans of action, bearing in mind that the individual is always at the center of the process.

Each of us is unique. We all have different life stories and are valuable in our own way. And we all have the great opportunity to commit to going through this transformation process. If we work on the components in the CSLM, we can safely make our way through a profound transformation process. At Gentera, we have used the model as a true guide, just as it has helped many people over recent years, people who can vouch for its efficacy. The goal is to implement the concept of Servant Leadership and become inspirational leaders, not just at Gentera but with people in every sphere of our lives.

In this era of technology and communications, constantly being bombarded with concepts and theories, the CSLM sheds it light on us, as a guide that helps us stay focused on its 11 components (Motivation, Values, Support System, Abilities, FISSEP, Sense of Purpose, Serving, Forming Others, Growing, Producing Results and Ethics), without losing sight of the central focus, which is ourselves. This is why the model takes the shape of a compass that tells us where our north is and points us in the direction we should be going.

> It doesn't matter
>
> what a leader thinks or feels
>
> but what he does, because
>
> actions are what produce results.

We already know that the first step in becoming an inspirational leader is self- knowledge, and because the individual is at the center of the process, we will begin by discussing self-knowledge as understood in the context of our model.

As we work on and develop each component of the CSLM, we will take stock of our progress and rethink our goals to ensure our lives remain in synch with our own personal Servant Leadership plan.

Each component of the model will be clearly defined along with its goals and practical advice on how to achieve them and measure our results. If we follow the model to the letter, we will have a greater chance of becoming inspirational leaders. Remember, it doesn't matter what a leader thinks or feels but what he does, because actions are what produce results.

"The Comprehensive Servant Leadership Model has helped give me structure, not just to be a better person but to lead more inspirationally."

Carlos Danel Cendoya, co-founder of Compartamos

"The Comprehensive Servant Leadership Model has made me receptive to feedback, but it has also enabled me to dare to give it. After all, it takes courage to give feedback to others. Getting to say the things you think and being able to understand others is extremely useful and valuable in making personal and professional relationships work well."

Ayleen Cortés, director of social responsibility and branding

"The Comprehensive Servant Leadership Model (CSLM) has been a guide for me, a discovery of the aspects that make up a person's life. Thanks to it, I have identified which parts of my life I need to develop. It has also helped me to create a life plan, both personal and professional, and to focus on what version of myself I want to continue to build."

Edna García, regional sales director

"The Comprehensive Servant Leadership Model is a compass you can use and regulate whenever you want. You can see the points and realize what you're neglecting. It's an excellent, easy-to-understand tool, both in theory and in practice. Plus, it's an ethically ironclad model. Projects need quality, caring people whose enthusiasm induces folks to join the endeavor of working according to the Comprehensive Servant Leadership Model. It's to everybody's benefit if we can share the advantages of being inspirational leaders. At Compartamos, we must not lose our capacity for being amazed at what we've done, and we must do our utmost to keep on amazing others.

Mario Alberto Gómez, regional sales director

"From the outset, the Comprehensive Servant Leadership Model seemed congruent to me. It's gone through changes and adjustments, but every time I look into it, analyze it, ponder it, it makes more sense to me. What we did was to put lifestyle on paper, as a sort of compass."

Horacio D'argence González, leadership

Self-Knowledge

Self-knowledge is at the heart of the inspirational leader. This reminds me of something I once read which contains a lot of truth: "Someone who doesn't know himself and doesn't know where he is headed cannot be an inspirational leader." What does this mean? Whenever we are asked, "How can I begin my own transformation?" or "How can I become an inspirational leader?, the same answer always comes to mind: self-knowledge.

If you can answer the following questions clearly and without hesitation, it means you have the makings of an inspirational leader and are in a position to further your personal growth. Who am I? What is my sense of purpose? What are my "whys"? What are my dreams and motivations? What are the values I live by? Who are the members of my support system? What are my abilities? What am I good at?

Before we can give to others, we need to know what we have to give, since no one can give what they don't have.

> "Man is the only creature that must learn who he is in order to be himself".
>
> J. Choza

Acquiring true self-knowledge requires dedication, time, effort and a great deal of soul searching. At Gentera, we place more value on acquiring self-knowledge than any Master's degree, course or professional project. Remember, we are people first and professionals second, and it would be very shortsighted of us not to acknowledge this and begin at the beginning. If your personal life is not in balance and harmonious and you are not aware of your motivations or don't have a sense of purpose, all your efforts in other areas will be in vain.

Once this is clarified, you can now start asking yourself the following questions: What are my priorities? What place do my anchors –such as God, my family and my health– hold in my life? If you put your mind to it, you can always find the time to work on self-knowledge, and the sooner the better! Nothing is more valuable to a real inspirational leader than being able to control your emotions and make the right decisions on your journey toward self-realization and fulfillment.

The Labyrinth

One of the tools that have served us most on our quest to gain self-knowledge is going into a labyrinth to meditate. To quote St. Augustine, "It is solved by walking", and nothing could be truer: the "hows" and their answers generally come to us along the way. According to experts, the first step is the most important one; by taking it, you will have achieved 30% of what you set out to accomplish.

Walking the labyrinth at Chartres Cathedral, in France, was a deeply enriching spiritual experience for me in terms of self-discovery. In fact, using labyrinths as a meditative tool dates back more than 4,000 years. A universal symbol of our pilgrimage through the journey that is life, labyrinths old and new can be found all over world, from France, Sweden and England to India, Peru and elsewhere in South America.

It is advisable to enter a labyrinth with a question or specific intention in mind, mainly focused on the questions Who am I? and Where am I headed? The goal is to see what has gone unseen and make your way to the center, walking at a pace conducive to meditation and reflection. Once you reach the center, you might want to stay there a while before making your way back. This type of single-path labyrinth is intended to help us concentrate, reflect, converse and commit to our self. There are no dead ends, no wrong turns. The only mystery to solve lies within us.

© Rectorat Cathédrale de Chartres

We recommend reading up on the subject and, most importantly, try and get the chance to walk one, because like spiritual retreats, it is a wonderful self-discovery tool and a great form of very active meditation.

Another useful way of acquiring self-knowledge is to get feedback from the people around us, especially our loved ones and those who have our interests at heart. A simple, yet effective feedback technique is the Situation-Behavior-Impact Model (SBI) developed by the Center for Creative Leadership (CCL).

Allow me to explain the three parts of this model. For feedback to be useful, we must first offer a brief description of the facts and context surrounding the situation, so the person receiving the feedback gets the message clearly.

The next step is to give a detailed description of the person's behavior in that situation and how events unfolded. This should be followed by observations on the impact of the person's behavior, i.e. the reactions or actions it provoked among third parties.

To ensure the efficacy of this technique, feedback should be timely and to the point. Also, it is recommended that for every negative comment, three positive ones be made, since it is more effective to focus on acceptable behaviors than to dwell on undesirable ones. Having a group of people whose feedback you can count on is an excellent means for growth.

> Flatter me, and I may not believe you.
>
> Criticize me, and I may not like you.
>
> Ignore me, and I may not forgive you.
>
> Encourage me, and I will not forget you.
>
> William Arthur

Beliefs and Paradigms

When you know what it is you want, you'll see it and things connected to it everywhere. And when you go looking for it, you'll find it. Some call it luck, but there's really no such thing as luck. Rather, it's the combination of three factors: knowing what you want, preparation and opportunity.

As we explore the subject of self-knowledge in greater depth, beliefs and paradigms crop up again and again, because sometimes we have to unlearn what we've been taught before we can learn something new. To make an analogy, if you want to fill a glass with water, the glass first has to have space and an opening.

I recall a specific experience that overturned one of my beliefs. I'd been told a thousand and one times that men can only do one thing at a time. So often had I heard it that I'd come to believe it. Yet in 2008, I ran a 42-kilometer marathon and as I ran, I listened to music, drank water, prayed the rosary, watched those running around me, kept track of my time and counted the kilometers. Who says men can only do one thing at a time?

> We are what we think.
>
> With our thoughts,
>
> we make the world.
>
> Buddha

There is a saying that goes: "You become what you think and what you believe you are." To illustrate this, let me give you the example of a heater: when we set the heater, say, to 77 degrees, the thermostat itself will make sure it reaches and stays at that temperature. In the event it gets hotter, it will automatically switch off, and if the temperature drops, it will turn back on. The same applies to our brains: if we program ourselves to be mediocre, that is exactly what we will always be. And when we begin to stand out above the average, something will happen or we will do something to sabotage ourselves, because in our minds we are programed to be average. Our thoughts and beliefs determined it to be so; we said it was so, and so it will be. That is why it is so important to question our paradigms and beliefs.

When I turned 40, I decided to put some of my beliefs and paradigms to the test, namely three whose common denominator was age. "You can't do that at your age! Don't be ridiculous!"

When I was a kid, I liked going to the circus to watch the unicycle acts and the clowns jump on the trampoline. Now, at 40, I had the chance to try my hand at both of these feats, so two of my challenges had to do with attempting something I'd loved as a child. The third challenge I set myself was finishing something I didn't think I could do and that I'd given up on a long time before: cracking the Rubik's Cube. I finally learned to ride a unicycle; I not only jumped on a trampoline but learned to do a backflip, and solved the Rubik's Cube. I proved it is possible to overturn our paradigms and beliefs, that these were self-imposed limitations.

The real challenge is to question our mistaken mentalities and find out if our beliefs and paradigms are still valid. In other words, is your inner dialogue right? Is it looking out for your best interests? Is it improving and protecting your health? Is it helping you achieve your goals and strengthening your sense of purpose?

To help us acquire greater self-knowledge, in addition to feedback from those around us, introspection and spiritual guidance, there are some useful tools and methodologies we can employ, like the Birkman Method, by Dr. Roger Birkman, and the Now, Discover Your Strengths test devised by Marcus Buckingham and Donald O. Clifton.

> "You can create your own circus. Choose the characters you want with you in life; choose the spot where you want to pitch your tent, and get on with the show."
>
> Daniela Villarreal, ballet dancer

On the subject of self-knowledge, there's also an illustrative story I'd like to share with you: Once in India, a thief who had stolen a gemstone worth a fortune was on the run from the police. They were about to catch him when the thief saw a beggar sleeping on the sidewalk. He slipped the gemstone into the sleeping man's pocket, his plan being to come back for it once he had given the police the slip, but a couple of streets along he was gunned down and died.

> The less I seem like it,
>
> the more I am.

The next day, the beggar got up and carried on with his life as usual. He never put his hand in his pocket, never discovered the precious stone that could have changed his life forever. Could it be that sometimes we neglect to look within ourselves and discover our own jewels, talents and gifts?

This story can be summed up as the less I seem like it, the more I am. To gain self-knowledge, we need to work on the components of internal dimension, in other words, our motivations, values, support system, abilities and FISSEP (physical, intellectual, social-family, spiritual and professional aspects), as well as our sense of purpose.

Self-knowledge is key to personal development and a lofty challenge, for getting to know ourselves is probably the hardest thing we'll ever do in life.

It requires being able to see ourselves for who we are, being able to acknowledge our weaknesses as well as our strengths, which, in turn requires humility. Without a sense of humility, it is virtually impossible to get to know ourselves. As St. Teresa of Avila said, "Humility is truth."

"To know myself, first of all, I have to be humble, lead a truthful life; see myself as I am in order to recognize my strengths and defects or weaknesses, and work on my main defect, relying on a life plan so I don't get off-track. I also have to work on my strengths in order to give my best and be the best version of myself."

Carlos Labarthe, co-founder of Compartamos

71

"Thanks to the self-knowledge work I've done, I've achieved insight into who I am, where I come from, what my strengths and weaknesses are. Without that, I wouldn't have been able to fully experience Gentera. I have seen thousands of concrete cases of transformation among collaborators and colleagues, but I'd like to talk about my own. My transformation has meant understanding where I am wounded; it's helped me to know myself better; understand where my fears are, my abilities, my areas of opportunity. In other words, what I'm good at."

Carlos Danel Cendoya, co-founder of Compartamos

"The FISSEP Model has given me and continues to allow me to know my point of balance, to keep in mind in which aspects of my life I am strong as well as which elements are fragile, with little work and with many opportunities for improvement, today I am fully confident that FISSEP is a formula to be Happy because it shows me exactly where I am standing and where I must start to find happiness, knowing myself through this model has been vital because today I have straightforward my strengths and where I can even help others as well as where I must allow myself to receive help to find the point of balance that gives Peace, Tranquility, Satisfaction, Self-realization.

Knowing and living the FISSEP model is like having found a direction in the path of life; it broke some paradigms, even some mirages, as well as knowing the different variables of Success, today it is clear to me that thanks to self-knowledge, I know perfectly what I want and what I don't, as well as what makes me fully Happy."

Rosalino Pozos, regional sales manager

"As an inspirational leader, the most valuable part of the learning process for me was learning to face up to my fears, the fears I'd always dodged. I confronted them, and that has bolstered my self-esteem, which gave me the courage to overcome them with courage, fortitude and knowledge. It is a tremendous transformation stemming from self-knowledge. This, along with working on forgiveness, has brought me a lot of peace."

Rosa Angélica Hernández Martínez, training manager

72

"The Comprehensive Servant Leadership Model enables me to know myself better. There are times when one is incongruent and we don't know ourselves. What makes us tick? What are our reactions? Where do our interests lie? It has also allowed me get to know my team, which has gone through the leadership programs. So, I know how to approach them and connect well with them."

Alfredo Zamora, executive director Business

"The Comprehensive Servant Leadership Model is totally balanced. It doesn't attempt to develop just one area of life but all of them. I think this model has served me on the professional side, on the spiritual level and in everything. It's very important now because we're growing a lot."

Mario Alberto Gómez, regional sales director

Internal Dimension. Component No. 1 Motivation

What inspires you?

The motivations of the inspirational leader are an important component of our CSLM model, but more than the motivations themselves, what we are concerned with is the extent of our knowledge of them: What is it that makes the inspirational leader tick? What inspires him? What powerful strengths drive him to do what he does?

Take, for instance, someone who is motivated by working with people. Something about it gives him a buzz, makes him feel happy and at peace all at the same time. We could say that working with others is one of his motivations, because he feels somehow that he is contributing to the development of the country and the world.

We all have our own motivations, and the emotions they give rise to are different for each of us.

> Inspirations come from inside each individual and are what move him to action.

It can be helpful to try and visualize our motivations as intrinsic, i.e. coming from within us; extrinsic, coming from external sources; or transcendental, which means they have an impact not just on ourselves, but on others.

> Motivations that combine
>
> pleasure and meaning
>
> can bring balance to our lives
>
> and will make us fully enjoy
>
> everything we do.

It is important to differentiate between different types of motivators, but for present purposes we will take them to be all those situations, places, causes, beliefs, environments, experiences and activities that bring out the best in us. Not just our family, friends or partners, but all contexts in which we flourish and can therefore make a more valuable contribution. Unlike external sources of motivation, we can say that intrinsic and transcendental motivations are inspired internally and drive us to accomplish things that are bigger than ourselves.

So where does inspiration come from? It comes from inside each individual and is what moves him to action. If it doesn't come from within, it is nothing more than a stimulus.

Often when people ask themselves "What motives me?", their initial responses will veer toward the material, be it a house, a car or some other possession, but if we dig a little deeper the answers tend to become more profound, like the desire to be a great leader or a better person. On an even deeper level, we find the motivation to transcend, to make a difference in an orphanage or working to eradicate poverty in vulnerable sectors of society. That is why we need to constantly question our motivations. If we ask ourselves why we do or aspire to something, this simple exercise will help us get to the root of our motivations and thus make delving into our self-knowledge easier.

Our most cherished dreams, the ones we are willing to sacrifice everything for, can shed a lot of light on our motivations in life. What are the dreams that keep you motivated and encourage others to dream? What is it that moves or inspires you?

> If our motivations are grounded solely in material things, we run the risk of going bankrupt.

Motivations that combine pleasure and meaning can bring balance to our lives and will make us fully enjoy everything we do. This, in turn, allows us to grasp the deeper meaning of making the right decisions. For example, if I have a job I enjoy and it's for a good cause, it will take on meaning because I'll know I'm helping. I'll find balance and will be motivated and inspired. The challenge, then, is to discover and be clear as to the motivations that inspire you and seek to incorporate them in your everyday life.

Some examples of motivation	
To be director some day	To learn
To own my own home	To serve others
To meet challenges	To go to heaven
To form a family	To save souls
To research	To become an inspirational leader
To dig for answers	To fight poverty

"Motivations are what get you moving, and when you do it, you feel fulfilled and ready to give it your all. My biggest lesson was finding out that what motivates me stems from my convictions. That's why, despite all the difficulties I might encounter, I know I can stay motivated because my convictions always keep me going."

Dulce Molina, leadership manager

"Throughout my life, I've had a lot of dreams, but like almost everyone, I forget about them or put them off. Thanks to the leadership programs, I've been able to get them back, get back in touch with them, explore them and understand that a person's sense of purpose in life changes over time, but the essence is the same. Things happen in life, children, for instance, that make you ask questions. The leadership programs afforded me space to ask myself whether each thing I'd attained or obtained was really what I had wanted, and about the way I've achieved it or how I'll achieve it in changing situations. Nowadays I relate all this to matters of priority. How do I want to spend my time?

Paulina Murguía Guerrero, corporate strategy

"The employees I have who attend the leadership programs come back highly motivated and open to change, which sharpens their decision-making skills. They come back ready to meet the challenges head-on."

Miguel Ángel Ortega Pacheco, regional sales director

"What motivates you? For sure, we all have lots of motivations, but the inspirational leader analyzes the reasons for each one and how it relates to Compartamos, which lets us self-regulate the leadership we want to exercise. When I first met some of the Compartamos founders, they painted me a sweet picture. Next thing I knew I was in a warehouse in Tapachula

sitting on a sack of beans and thinking, 'I bought into a dream.' But work carried the day, and that's how I learned that the way you tell others what you really want requires the right degree of energy, emotion and clarity. Therein lies your ability to invite them to join in on this tremendous project."

Mario Alberto Gómez, regional sales director

Internal Dimension. Component No. 2 Values

What guides you?

Every inspirational leader defines and, most importantly, lives by the values he holds dearest. It is in our nature to live by universal values, and generally speaking, we try and uphold them.

> Values safeguard human
>
> dignity. They are not subject
>
> to the whims of time or place.

Based on this premise, we need to take stock of which values are most important to us and live up to them. A value system is a moral compass that points the conduct and lives of individuals and social groups in the direction of self-realization and that is capable of bringing about social transformation and, ultimately, happiness.

Values safeguard human dignity. They are not subject to the whims of time or place; there are no half measures, no shades of gray: either you live by them or you don't. At this point, we need to stop and ask ourselves: What are the values that govern our lives, the ones we are not willing to compromise on, no matter what? Which values do I want to commit to? But values are pointless unless we translate them into concrete actions, both in our professional and private lives. Try and identify which values you'd like people to think of when they hear your name. You might be able to think of three or four or maybe just one, but what are they? In other words, what does our value hierarchy look like when it comes to putting them into action? An inspirational leader lives by his values, so once we're clear on which ones govern our lives, the easier it will be to aspire to becoming one.

Today more than ever it's very important to define our values clearly, put them into practice and ensure others respect them. Generally speaking, modern society takes a more relaxed moral outlook and would appear to be obsessed with pleasure rather than happiness.

Some examples of values	
Responsibility	Modesty
Punctuality	Order
Freedom	Loyalty
Humility	Justice
Moderation	Moderation
Industriousness	Prudence
Generosity	Perseverance
Sincerity	Austerity
Respect	Authenticity
Honesty	Tenacity

"Values are what definitely keep you on-track in life. I didn't have a father figure, so my values come from my mother and from a person who was close to me in my early years. When I was 12, my mother and I had to move into a tenement where you'd see people getting drunk and doing drugs in broad daylight. Crime and violence were commonplace. I lived there for three years, precisely the age when you're trying to figure things out and you're vulnerable to falling in with those around you, but thank God I got out of there without picking up negative behaviors. Taking stock, I figure it was

due to the values my mother instilled in me and constantly reinforced. Without that, I don't know what would have become of me."

Gonzalo Ramírez, leadership

Internal Dimension. Component No. 3 Support System

Who is in your support system?

The inspirational leader needs the support of a group of people who know, understand and care about him; people he can trust and who will be there for him in his time of need, in sickness and in health, for richer or for poorer, for better or for worse.

Building, maintaining and nurturing a support system speaks to the intelligence and humility of the inspirational leader who realizes he can't always go it alone, that sometimes he needs help.

The concept is simple, but at the same time it's not always easy to acknowledge that we're only human and that we're going to need help at some point in the future. That help is vital if we want to become inspirational leaders, so we need to build, maintain and take care of our support system.

> "If you want to go fast, go alone; if you want to go far, go with another."
> African proverb

Self-preservation is a quality that requires humility, just as it takes humility to ask for help when we need it. In the case of a leader, a sense of self-preservation is even more important because it means he isn't just thinking of himself. Picture, for example, a group of mountaineers on an expedition. A member of the group is exhausted but doesn't say so. By failing to speak up, he not only puts himself at risk but endangers the lives of all the other members of the team.

This is why it's perfectly valid for a leader to say, "I can't", "I don't know" or "I don't want to." This is what self-preservation is all about. It doesn't mean we shouldn't take on challenges. It just means we should take on only challenges of our choosing, and this is where the support system comes in, to help us deal with situations that, even as leaders, we can't handle on our own.

It should be noted, however, that support systems don't just "spring up out of nowhere". They require hard work and effort; they are built on a daily basis and should never be taken for granted. To say, for example, "They're my family, so they have to help me" doesn't always hold true, since support systems we hold as "natural" or "logical" aren't always the ones that work adequately. Often we require the help of people outside the family setting, maybe a good doctor, lawyer, priest, banker or friends who have skills or knowledge of their own to contribute in different ways.

Inspirational leaders, as we perceive them, take the time to choose their support systems. You need to choose the people who will help you the most to grow and learn every day. Do you know who you'd pick to sit on your "personal board of directors"?

Equally important is to let everyone in your support system know how they contribute to your life and what they mean to you. They should be aware of what you need and expect from them. Ideally, they should be people who know and care about you, who have a certain quality or ability you need or that can be of use to you.

> The secret to real,
>
> permanent change is
>
> to have a good support system.

Often after taking a course or reading a book or, more commonly, on New Year's Eve or after an eye-opening experience, we promise ourselves we'll change for the better. We resolve to improve our relationship with our spouse or family, start exercising, eat healthier, be a better person, a better leader and things along these lines. Yet for some inexplicable reason, our resolve weakens over time, and we find ourselves back at square one, angry and frustrated.

The secret to real, permanent change is to have a good support system. The most important element in your plan of action is knowing who is there for you, who will be there to support you, guide you, offer you feedback, teach you.

You need to create a new context, surround yourself with key people who will comprise your support system. These should be people who bring out the best in you and who have only your best interests at heart. It is very important they are familiar with your goals and why you want to achieve them. If you have a good support system, even in trying times you will always have a source of motivation and encouragement.

It is vital that you be accompanied throughout the process. It's not magic; it's just a matter of making the decision, obtaining the means, paying the price and being willing to make the effort. Of course there are things you'll have to leave behind. If you want to reach your final destination, you're going to have to lighten the load, get your priorities straight and visualize yourself living the life you want to lead. And soon you will be, if you use the proper means to get there. With faith, a good support system and God in the center, anything is possible. Success guaranteed!

Your support system is comprised of people you need and who support you, but how do you thank them and what will you have to give them in return? You also need to identify which people can't or won't want to support you in certain situations. This is another skill you need to develop.

The Jar of Life

Let me use a metaphor to illustrate my point. I call it "the jar of life". Let's imagine for a moment that our lives are represented by a huge jar that contains our entire existence, in which our day-to-day responsibilities, the ones that absorb most of our time and energy, like work, paying the rent, maintaining the house and car, etc., are represented by stones. These stones take up maybe 75% of the jar, while the remaining 25% is taken up with sand, which represents the dreams, plans and projects that are always at the back of our minds, like that vacation we've always dreamed of or that special something we've been wanting to buy, etc. The jar of life, it would seem, is full.

> The Comprehensive Servant Leadership Model
> provides a great chance to refill our jar of life.

And this is how we spend our lives, with packed agendas, one engagement after the other and endless activities. But at some point amid all the coming and going, we start to despair. We feel we are not making progress, that we are still far from realizing our dreams, or worse, we start to feel empty and dissatisfied. Then we remember there are other stones we have to find room for in the jar, the big ones, the anchors: health, family, God. But the jar is already full, and we begin to feel overwhelmed. We feel we don't have enough time for everything, and no matter how hard we try, the results we are after are unattainable and our lives lack balance and harmony.

The Comprehensive Servant Leadership Model offers us the great opportunity to refill our jar of life, the chance to reorder our priorities in life.

In this brand new jar, we suggest you place the biggest stones, the anchors –God, family and health– at the bottom, as a foundation. These stones will keep the jar stable, and even if nothing else turns out as we expect, these anchors will be enough to ensure our sense of balance and purpose remain intact. Next come the smaller stones that represent our day-to-day activities –work, paying the rent, maintaining our car and home, etc.–, and everything starts to make sense, because these stones fit neatly in the spaces between the bigger stones. Now that the jar is almost full, it's time to add the sand –our dreams, plans and projects–, which fills every nook and cranny between the big stones and the smaller ones. Only this way can we make use of all the available space in the jar of life and lead full, rewarding lives. But there is one element missing: water, which represents solidarity, brotherly love and time devoted to giving, serving and inspiring others. As we pour the water into the jar, we can see how it flows over the stones, refreshing them and taking the hardness off their edge; how it seeps into the sand and opens up spaces that appeared compact and impenetrable.

Thus our lives are not only full and rewarding, but they take on transcendence. The new arrangement represents the lifestyle of an inspirational leader, who is essentially God's helper.

The jar is a practical way of illustrating how we should organize our support system. I recommend watching the video Rocks in a Jar.

Some examples of support values
My co-worker, Pedro Juárez, always encourages and inspires me when it comes to my projects.
My wife, María Jiménez, loves me and listens to me without judging me. She is always there for me.
My friend, Rubén Solís, questions me, and his honesty helps me grow and dream.
My spiritual guide points me in the right direction.
Someone who has the abilities you'd like to develop.

"The support system is a kind of CSLM anchor, which means it's a great help for anyone. It is a small group of people who give you a hand in your process of building a better human being. I think it's important to have people from the various spheres in which we evolve, for instance, family members like

your wife, your father or mother, brother or sister, among others, who see how you behave and what role you play in the family. Also, folks you work with or who are in the company where you're developing, because it's important that your support system has people who see you performing on the job, like your leader, a colleague or fellow team members. And you also need somebody who is not family or job related. It depends on what you're looking for, but to me, ideally, it could be a spiritual guide, a coach or a friend. The main thing is that you fully trust that person so that you can share your CSLM, your life plan, your concerns and the challenges that lay ahead.

Carlos Labarthe, co-founder of Compartamos

"My wife is my primary support system. I really like talking with her about my plans and goals, especially if they're complex and present major challenges. I know she's always there to cheer me on or get me back in line if I get off track. Taking stock of my achievements, in large part they are due to her. What I'm most grateful for is that thanks to her I've grown closer to God. Before knowing her, I'd completely gotten away from the church; I never went to mass, and the only sacrament I'd received was baptism. When we decided to get married, it put me in a tough situation. Thanks to her loving support, I studied catechism for a whole year, to take my first communion and be confirmed, and then I was ready to get married. Every day she could she'd go along with me and help me. I never missed a class, and from then on my life changed radically."

Gonzalo Ramírez, leadership

"Understanding what the Support System means has helped me to understand the two sides of the coin: on the one hand, to ask for help, to have someone to turn to at all times, and on the other hand, to be someone else's support system."

Juan Manuel Zurita, regional sales director

"Cultivating a support system based on our model sends us a message that highlights other factors. It shows us that no matter how much we fancy ourselves leaders, we need others, and that's where this factor's significance and beauty lie. In acknowledging and working within a support system, we accept ourselves as being vulnerable, and that paradoxically makes us stronger. Christ himself worked for three years with his own support system: his disciples. With them he grew, cried, matured and got stronger. He passed on a huge lesson in humility. In the leadership programs, we encourage and value the transcendence of voluntarily and individually constructing every one of our personal networks, which lets us keep on learning and will lovingly take an interest in us, sustaining and fortifying us in attaining our deepest yearnings and dreams.

Hugo Cantú, leadership

Internal Dimension. Component No. 4: Capacities

What are you good at?

At Gentera, we have a saying: "We're all tied by the same rope," and nothing could be truer. The inspirational leader needs to identify and acknowledge not just his capacities but his God-given gifts, and put them to the services of others.

We're all born with capacities that we're called to use and build on. It is our responsibility to discover them through an honest, deep process of introspection. Who better than ourselves to identify and define those talents that make us feel good when we use them; that make us feel we are giving the best of ourselves to others and to life when we put them to the service of a project, our family, our colleagues or the world in general?

Yet this discovery and recognition process isn't always easy. Surprisingly, in practice, it is often the people around us who recognize our gifts and capacities, in which case it is important to have the humility to receive feedback and the courage to be brutally honest with ourselves.

> We're all tied
>
> by the same rope.

To help us define our strengths, it is useful to ask ourselves what comes naturally to us. What things do I do well or exceptionally well? In which areas do I generally receive positive feedback? In other words, what am I good at? How do I know I'm good at it? It's important to gather tangible, quantifiable evidence so as to avoid falling prey to unfounded beliefs or paradigms.

If you had the confidence you wouldn't fail at something because you have the capacity to do it, what would you do? The next question is: Why don't you do it?

Some examples of capacities	
Being a good listener	Being creative
Getting good prices	Ordering your ideas
Being able to forgive and move on	Taking pictures
Composition	Building things
Finishing what you started	Cooking
Coming up with lots of new ideas	Public speaking
Being good with words or handling groups	Teaching people
Motivating people	Organizing trips
Analyzing and summarizing	Running marathons
Manual skills	Offering consolation

"Our capacities are our strengths. Clearly, we're not good at everything or bad at everything. Some things we do extremely well and those are our capacities. If we can't identify our capacities or strengths, it's a big help to ask our support system. People who see us in action, either with family members or on the job, are well aware of what we're good at. In general, what we're good at comes naturally to us. When I began to make my CSLM, it was a big help to ask my wife from her point of view what she thought I was good at; what I do really well. I did the same with my co-workers at Gentera. It's very important to recognize our capacities, because that will help us grow in the future, as our foundation for growth is our strengths, which we emphasize and strengthen to achieve the best version of ourselves."

Carlos Labarthe, co-founder of Compartamos

"As for capacities, I have to say I designed executive development programs for over 30 years. However, Compartamos requires experiential education capacities that demanded acquiring new experiences and knowledge, which obliged me to learn new adult education techniques at my 54 years of age. Today, I feel fulfilled for being able to contribute to forming inspirational leaders. You never know when life is going to demand that you learn new skills, so cultivating an attitude of never-ending learning is basic."

José Luis Núñez, leadership

> The secret to a good cup of coffee
> is in the blend.

Are you leading a well-rounded life?

The Gentera philosophy establishes an unwavering commitment to the individual, and in response to this genuine interest, we have created a blueprint to promote a culture of comprehensive development, which, in turn, will put us firmly on the path to a full, happy and healthy life. Our blueprint forms part of our Comprehensive Servant Leadership Model (CSLM) and takes into account the (Spanish initials for Family, Intellectual, Mental and Physical Health, Social, Spiritual and Professional aspects), hence its acronym, as well as our support system and sense of purpose.physical, intellectual, social-family, spiritual and professional (FISSEP, for its Spanish acronym) aspects of the individual, without forgetting that these are all interrelated; that growth in one area will depend on growth in another. We need to determine what our goals are in each of these areas and learn to balance them if we are to lead successful, rewarding lives.

They say the secret to a good cup of coffee is in the blend, and there can be no denying we can't give what we don't have. This is why we need to start by working on ourselves, by asking ourselves if we are leading rounded lives with a sense of purpose and a clear direction. In other words, do I know what I want to achieve in each FISSEP area of my life? Have I drawn up a plan of action?

After asking ourselves these questions, we are free to choose between taking action and continuing to live our lives on automatic pilot as we have been. In short, the goal is to live a full, intense life, one we can share with others and that allows us to leave a legacy.

Only by living well-rounded FISSEP lives will we be in a condition to give fully to others, to share who we are and what we have learned with them. This is the path to transcendence.

---

[17] Spanish acronym of Physical, Intellectual, Social-family, Spiritual and Professional (FISSEP).

> I am the master of my fate. I am the
>
> captain of my soul.
>
> William Ernest Henley

The Balancing Act of FISSEP

If we approach the problem logically, we'll never make any headway. There simply aren't enough hours in the day. The only way to achieve a balance in every aspect of our lives is to integrate them, which basically means to "unify all the parts".

A lifestyle in which all FISSEP aspects are integrated is just the one we live all the time, at every moment, no matter where we are or who we are with. But to live such a lifestyle, we first need a well-defined sense of purpose. We need to be aware of our values and motivations, know what our dreams are. And once we do, we'll know exactly what we want to achieve in each area of our lives. We'll be clear on our priorities and will walk, compass in hand, to our final destination.

Remember that every day we either come closer to realizing our dreams or stray farther away from them. By leading a life that integrates all FISSEP dimensions, you will be taking firm giant steps toward materializing your dreams. There are no shortcuts in life, only plans of action.

Indubitably, this is a personal decision, and we are all free to choose how we want to live our lives and steer our fate. By the same token, however, there can be no denying that the ability to integrate all these facets of our lives is what differentiates average folk from successful leaders who inspire others.

We are extremely fortunate to be privy to this "secret" and to have the means and support to carry it out. We've all been warned that opportunity only comes knocking once, but at the end of the day, as William Ernest Henley so succinctly puts in his poem "Invictus": "I am the master of my fate. I am the captain of my soul."

We mustn't forget that any number multiplied by zero is zero, and the same applies to the FISSEP dimensions of our lives. For example, if my health is zero, even if I'm doing well in other areas, the end result will be zero. To better grasp this concept, let's look at each dimension individually.

Family dimension. The traditional family is the ideal place for the development of a person because, in it, we are loved; we learn to love and act based on values. This is why we value the family and are committed to it. In doing so, we promote the formation of better families that strengthen and create a better country and a better society. And there is no doubt that a well-grounded and cohesive family is the foundation of society.

Intellectual dimension. Knowledge enables us to develop the intellectual abilities and values that afford us the tools to form better criteria, broaden our cultural base and apply it to all aspects of our lives.

Physical and mental health dimension. Physical health consists of physical activities and practices that promote health and integration between you and your family members, such as vacations, food, rest, exercise, and sports. For example, the day has 24 hours, and an average person sleeps eight hours, representing one-third of the day. Imagine now that you are 60, meaning 20 of your 60 years, you have been sleeping. Consider what would have happened if instead of sleeping eight hours, you had slept seven; at 60, you would have slept 17.5 years instead of 20, meaning you would have two and a half more years to do what you wanted. Imagine 2.5 full years, with days and nights reading, volunteering, spending time with your children and wife, or praying. 2.5 more years of waking life. Mental health is a fundamental part of health and wellness that underpins our individual and collective abilities to make decisions, build relationships and shape our world. Mental health is also a basic human right and essential for personal, community, and socioeconomic development.

Social dimension. Recognizing the person as a social being who depends on others and everything surrounding them is essential to developing and establishing healthy interpersonal relationships. We can create a culture of cooperation, help, and solidarity towards those most in need, based on volunteer activities or social aid type, from our knowledge and understanding of the social realities that exist in our country.

Spiritual dimension. We at Gentera are convinced that families that pray together stay together. We believe a harmonious relationship with God is essential if we are to live in peace with ourselves and others. To achieve this, we should engage in spiritually enriching practices and activities, such as attending spiritual retreats, going to mass, helping others, meditating, praying, etc. In other words, we view the spiritual dimension as the cornerstone of our lives, the driving force that sparks intelligence and willpower, allowing us to be close to God. Only by knowing and loving God can we undertake and tolerate anything.

Professional dimension. This dimension has to do with how to develop professional capacities and skills, draw up a career plan and devote means to developing the areas needed to progress in the workplace and in life. Work, be it of a vocational or professional nature, is a valid means of self-realization.

> You decide how you want to finish your life, planning or in a nosedive.
>
> Javier Santiago.18

---

[18] Mexican athlete, silver medal winner in the 2010 run-up (racing upstairs) world championship.

A FISSEP analysis tells us exactly where we stand vis-à-vis the most important aspects of life, so that we can come up with plans to foster our growth in each of these areas.

To reach equilibrium and balance, a leader must work intensely and committedly on many areas: on what is formal and informal, on professional and personal issues, as well as on curricular and extra curricular matters. Inspirational leaders must create their own contexts and make the time to reflect, assimilate and apply what they have learned.

Some examples of of FISSEP-based questions that shed light on our level of commitment
Family: How is my relationship with my family?
Intellectual: How much time do I devote to learning and researching?
Physical and mental health: How much sleep do I get, how is my health, how many vacations do I take?
Spiritual: How is my relationship with God?
Professional: How updated am I professionally? How conscientiously do I follow up on my career plan?

"A little over three years ago I was so ill I almost died. Within myself, I saw the Compartamos machinery working for me. Throughout the month or so I was out of commission, the prayer chains were constant. The whole

Compartamos family, all the leadership, put themselves at an employee's service. That's priceless. I could see that leadership they talk about in action. I lived it in the flesh, so I know it's not just a slogan. It was very impressive, and I'm grateful. It's also been meaningful to find the means to overcome fears, become aware and do things you never thought you could do. The Comprehensive Servant Leadership Model brings out the best in us so that after we've done something, we wonder how we accomplished what we thought was impossible. And that changes your limits, your life."

Alfredo Zamora, executive director Business

"In my case, I have almost 16 years in this institution, the Comprehensive Servant Leadership Model (CSLM) formed my adult life, and the experience of FISSEP has helped me always to seek to be integral and not to neglect anything within my integrity as a person and as a leader, we always know that as people we have different challenges in life and when we take the CSLM and FISSEP as a guide or compass things always go better. I am calmer when I stop and plan my life. A life plan I made some years ago based on the FISSEP has allowed me to improve daily; there is always room for improvement. Still, the reality is that having my life plan based on the MIS and FISSEP I owe the person I am today to it."

Haniel Cárdenas, regional sales director

"As for the physical aspect, I recall a specific situation that allowed me to experience an example of what FISSEP means. We'd just finished a tough day at work, but the boss said, 'Let's take advantage of our time.' And I asked him, 'How are we going to take advantage of our time if we've gone down the checklist and we've done everything?' To which he replied, 'It's time to take care of the physical side," and we went out to exercise. That's part of FISSEP: to get done with one aspect and take up another that's equally important. It's a part of the whole. It's obvious that you've got to thank God, life and the company, for the opportunity and also for being able to count on a phase of support such as the leadership programs. It's a golden opportunity that shows us we must always inspire employees to work not only on the professional aspect but on all the FISSEP aspects."

"FISSEP has helped me with everything. Personally, it's helped me guide my daughter, listen to her better. I feel my advice is more pertinent for her these days. The chats my husband and I have at least once a week over coffee are more satisfying. Professionally, I have the tools to be more tolerant, more of an advisor and more adept at finding the path to Servant Leadership. I've also been empowered in terms of my health and in my social life, because FISSEP helps me stay balanced."

Rosa Angélica Hernández Martínez, training

"FISSEP helps you find out how you form and can create (virtuous) circles. For instance, I go on a diet and do exercise. I want to be healthy. I get on the treadmill, and my kids automatically follow me; my wife, too. You can't help but influence your surroundings. People congratulate you and do good things without you having to ask them."

Horacio D'argence González, leadership

> "The purpose of life is
> a life of purpose".
> Robert Byrne

Internal Dimension. Component No. 6 Sense of Purpose

Where are you headed? Why? What for?

This is an essential component of the Comprehensive Servant Leadership Model and is related to the task of discovering what our calling in life is and fulfilling it. It requires acknowledging we have the ability to transcend, to fulfill our sense of purpose, and this can only be done on a day-to-day basis. Generally speaking, a leader's sense of purpose transcends him and engages other people. In other words, the challenge is to lead our lives with a defined purpose. And to the extent we are clear on our "what fors", the easier it will be to accomplish our mission in life.

It is very important to know "why" we do what we do and "what for". Everything we do and say should be backed by a "what for" and a sense of purpose.

The "what fors" are our dreams, the "hows" are the actions we take to realize them, and the "whats" are the results of those actions.

Metaphorically, this component could be described as a path. On the first stretch, we discover our sense of purpose in life. It might take some of us longer than others to travel it, but it's a process we should not and cannot evade if we aspire to be inspirational leaders.

Continuing with the same metaphor, once we've discovered our vocation and mission, our calling in life, based on our motivations, values and capacities, the second part of the path is to align our day-to-day actions with our sense of purpose.

A sense of purpose should come hand-in-hand with an appreciation of the things we have rather than focusing on what we want. When we manage to detach ourselves from desire and cling instead to the things in life that are of genuine value, we will become the best possible versions of ourselves.

> A sense of purpose is an open road
>
> to be discovered and traveled.
>
> Every obstacle, every effort,
>
> every step we take along the way
>
> should be assessed and savored.

If we don't have a sense of purpose, if we don't question ourselves and discover what it is, life will decide for us. Obviously, we will have to reevaluate our sense of purpose periodically in light of our circumstances and depending on where we are in our lives, which requires constant reflection so we can determine what changes we need to make and in which direction to head with each passing milestone.

If we want to jump across a puddle without getting wet, what do we focus on: our feet, the puddle or the other side of the puddle where we want to land? If we focus on the puddle, where do you think we're going to land? This is why we need a sense of purpose in life, why we need to keep our sights set on the path ahead, always keeping in mind the premise, "I'm going where I look."

At this point, it is useful to take stock of where we are today and how far we have come. We need to ask ourselves why we do what we do and if at the end of the day our actions are aligned with our mission in life.

Put differently, rather than a goal, a sense of purpose is an open road to be discovered and traveled. Every obstacle, every effort, every step we take along the way should be assessed and savored in the knowledge that we are honoring our existence and making a difference in the world, because we are putting our sense of purpose into practice every waking moment.

I believe a sense of purpose should be as powerful as the one that inspired us to found Compartamos or our goal of reaching one million customers.

100

In my own particular case, my dream was so motivating and my "what for" so transcendental that I got the courage to smash paradigms and overturn personal beliefs. Armed with that inspirational sense of purpose and accompanied by the Gentera motto "Anything is possible!" I have managed to lead a full, rewarding and happy life, and hopefully have made a difference in the lives of others.

The day we reached that great goal of serving one million clients coincided with Saint Teresa's birthday. And that was how it was meant to be: a special, meaningful day. It was also a historic one for Mexico, because it was the day we won the "gold medal in micro-finances".

Looking back on the experience, I am reminded that the journey is more important than the final destination. It is the process that brings us happiness, something we would do well to bear in mind in today's instant-pleasure-seeking society.

Clearly, having meaningful goals is essential to maintain happiness, but we shouldn't lose sight of the fact that when we set ourselves goals, we are really writing our own story before it actually happens. A powerful goal is a dream with a deadline.

Some statistics that illustrate our level of success and evidence the fact that we have realized our dream
Co-workers: 5,558
Offices serving the public: 301
Sales departments: 2
Assistant sales departments: 6
Regions: 35
Active Portfolio: $5,121,144,265.62 (Mexican pesos)
Clients: 1,007,496

Circumstances and contexts may change along the way, and life might not give us everything we ask for, but it always gives us what we need, provided we have a clear, updated sense of purpose, enthusiasm and passion.

> He who has a why to live for
>
> can bear almost any how.
>
> Friedrich Nietzche

What scares us is the light, not darkness. Some people set themselves up for failure because they are afraid of success. For others, death can be more exciting than life: being aware of our mortality reminds us we should make the most of the gift of life.

We need to ask ourselves, what makes us feel alive? And once we have an answer, we need to get out there and do it. This world needs people who are truly alive.

Fear is a bigger killer than death. If you feel unmotivated, try and pinpoint what it is you're afraid of and why. You'll be surprised at the outcome.

There is a story about some Japanese fishermen who used to fish very close to the water's edge. For a long time, they caught a lot of fish this way, until circumstances changed with the arrival of more fishermen. And so they were forced to sail further out to sea to catch the same amount of fish. This worked for a while, but before long their customers started complaining that the fish weren't as fresh as before, so they took along refrigerators, but their customers noticed the difference in flavor and complained. So they built enormous pools aboard their ships to keep the fish alive until they reached shore. It seemed like an excellent solution, until they noticed some fish had become lazy. Realizing they had no predators, they simply floated in the pool or stopped moving altogether. The fishermen's customers noticed they had a bitter taste. So the fishermen came up with another idea: they introduced a couple of sharks into the pools to keep the fish on the alert and in constant movement. Finally, their customers were satisfied and the fishermen learned a valuable lesson: leaving behind the comfort zone and entering the challenge zone makes us more productive, fills us with enthusiasm and passion and reinforces our sense of purpose. Is it time you introduced a couple of sharks into your life?

> "The Beatles remind us that the essence of any successful organization is small teams of individuals who do things they love, have fun together, and feel part of a greater whole while maintaining their individual identities."
>
> Andrew Sobel

Difficulties and obstacles will always be there, waiting for us at every turn, but when we turn to face the sun, our shadow falls behind us. Our sense of purpose is, then, our compass.

This completes the components of our internal dimension. The sixth, our sense of purpose, will emerge as a logical consequence of having discovered, meditated on, developed and interiorized the other five.

Once we have acquired this level of self-knowledge, we can move on to the next phase, which is our external dimension. At this point, we are ready to give to others and inspire them to live meaningful lives.

Let's not forget that someone who has a "reason to live" can take the "how", no matter how hard, which brings to mind an anecdote about two bricklayers. On the surface, it appeared the two men were engaged in the same activity: for hours on end, they laid layer after layer of bricks and mortar. A man went over to one of them and asked, "What are you doing?" The bricklayer replied, "Building a wall." The man then turned to the other bricklayer and asked him the same thing. The man smiled and said, "I'm building a cathedral so thousands of pilgrims can come from all over the country to give glory to our Lord God."

Clearly, the two men had very different senses of purposes, even though they appeared to be working toward the same objective. It would be good

103

if we could question our sense of purpose and that of the people around us before the day is out. You never know… you might be surprised or you might even learn something interesting.

I remember giving a talk on the subject at an event once. There were some 70 couples in the room, and before I launched into my speech on the importance of having a sense of purpose, I asked them to share their dreams with each other, the ones that were most important to them. Minutes later I asked the people who had known their spouse's dream to raise their hands. I was shocked to see only seven hands. Seven people out of 140! How can we allow this to happen? How can we not be aware of the dreams of the person we love and share our life with?

5–10–15 Exercise

This exercise is intended to help us define our purpose in life and project it into the future. A lot of the people who have done the exercise have found it useful. Personally, it's given me a lot of ideas and encouraged me to take concrete action.

Simply draw five columns on a sheet of paper. In the first column, write the names of your loved ones; in the second, write their current age; in the third, their current age plus five years; in the fourth, their current age plus ten years, and in the last column, their current age plus 15 years.

Next, try and imagine what your loved ones will look like when they reach the ages in each column and how the family dynamic will have changed. Maybe your children will be at university or maybe they'll be married. Your parents might be getting on or even have passed away. The columns help us visualize different scenarios and identify our priorities so we can start planning for the future. We can decide which actions we need to take today and what can wait. For example, whether we need to save and if so, how much. Or how much free time we're going to need and when.

Once we've explored all the possible scenarios, we will be in a better position to determine where we stand today and where we want to be in five, ten or 15 years. Wouldn't you like to become an inspirational leader in this time?

If you do this exercise using your own family, it will immediately become evident that our responsibilities vary depending on what stage in life we're at. It also gives us an idea of what the family dynamic will be like in the near future. In my case, my two kids will either have finished or have almost finished university, which means I need to spend the next few years saving. I need to try to visualize what I'll be doing, what my role will be, if I'll have the energy and health to meet the challenges that are likely to come my way in five, ten or 15 years, if I need to make time for my parents and the other relatives I care about now instead of waiting for the "perfect" moment. It all comes down to statistics and being able to adapt and revise our sense of purpose with the passing of time. If we can visualize possible scenarios, we will be better equipped to take on the future.

	Today	In 5 years	In 10 years	In 15 years
Iván	44	49	54	59
Chriss	37	42	47	52
Lorenzo	16	21	26	31
Gonzalo	15	20	25	30
Marcelo	7	12	17	22

Examples of a sense of purpose:
Help Christ and do His work among the poorest of the poor." Saint Teresa of Calcutta
"Contribute to interracial inclusion in the United States." Martin Luther King
"Help others find meaning in their lives." Viktor Frankl
"Go to heaven." Carlos Labarthe
"Have a Kia Kaha family." Iván Mancillas

The Tuna Fisherman

"Happiness is a path, not a destination." And what better way to illustrate this phrase than the story of the tuna fisherman. It all began when an investment banker bumped into a fisherman at the pier of a small fishing village in Mexico. At the bottom of the fisherman's boat were several good-sized yellowfin tuna fish. The banker complimented the fisherman on the quality of his fish and asked him how long it had taken him to catch them. "Not long," the fisherman replied. So the banker asked him why he didn't stay out at sea longer and catch more fish, to which the fisherman replied that the fish he had caught were sufficient to meet his family's immediate needs.

"And what do you do with the rest of your time?" asked the banker. To which the fisherman replied, "I sleep until late, fish a little, play with my kids, take a nap with my wife María, and every night I go into town and have a drink and play guitar with my friends. In short, I have a busy, enjoyable life."

"I'm a graduate of Harvard University and have a Master's in Finance and Administration. I can help you," said the banker. "You should devote more time to fishing and with the extra money you earn, you could buy a bigger boat and with the income from the bigger boat you could buy more boats and build up a whole fleet. Then, instead of selling your catch to a broker you could sell it directly to a processing plant and in time, you could even open your own processing plant. Of course you'd have to oversee production, operation and distribution, which would mean leaving this small town and moving to the city, so you could manage your rapidly expanding company."

"And how long would it take me to do all that?" asked the fisherman. "15 to 20 years," said the banker. And the fisherman said, "Why would I want to wait so long and work so hard?" The banker laughed. "When the time comes, you can issue an IPO (Initial Public Offering) and sell your company's shares to the public. You'd be rich. You'd have millions," he said. "Millions and then what?" asked the fisherman. "Then you could retire. You could move to a small town on the coast and sleep until late, fish a little, play with your kids, take a nap with your wife, go into town every night and have a drink and play guitar with your friends." "Isn't that what I do now?" replied the fisherman.

Moral: How many people waste their lives chasing happiness when it's right under their noses? True happiness is appreciating what we have and not bemoaning what we're lacking. If we cry over losing the sun, our tears will keep us from being able to see the stars.

> "If a man does not know to what port he is steering, no wind is favorable to him."
>
> Seneca

People who constantly ask themselves "what for?" find God. He comes to meet us when we're able to stop and reflect on our actions. Only by questioning ourselves over and over again can we discover our true sense of purpose.

One of my dreams, one of the things that give my life a sense of purpose is to turn my family into a *Kia Kaha* family, a strong, loyal family that has its place in heaven assured. This is why I aspire to be God's helper. And if I had to give a job description, I'd say it's no different from being an inspirational leader.

When I meditate on Jesus' sense of purpose, I realize it was to carry out his Father's plan and obey his will. And when I think of my own sense of purpose, I realize I need God to help me discover what it is and fulfill my mission in this world. I need his help to find meaning in my life. I just wish things were as clear for me as they were for Jesus, who was filled with so much love there was no doubt in his mind.

> If we don't enjoy what we're doing, then we're doing something wrong.

Luckily, it's easy to know if you're on the right track or not: if we don't enjoy what we're doing, if we don't feel fulfilled and happy, we're doing something wrong. And now that we're on the subject of sense of purpose, there's a story I'd like to tell you. Once a father went to wake his son up for school like he did every morning. That morning the door was closed, so he knocked several times. "It's six in the morning. Time to get up and go to school," said the father. "I'm not going," said the son. "What do you mean, you're not going? Get up and open the door," said the father. To which the son replied that he had three reasons not to go: school was boring, the kids bullied him and the teachers hated him.

"I also have three reasons why you should go," said the father. "First, it's your duty; second, you're 45; and third, you're the school principal."

Which goes to show there are no fair winds for people who don't know where they're headed. This is why it's so important to analyze, understand and appropriate the components of our external dimension, which are to serve and form others, grow and produce results. These are the commitments undertaken by the inspirational leader. Remember, no one can give what (s)he doesn't have.

⊕

"Comprehensive Servant Leadership Model (CSLM) has helped me find my sense of purpose by first helping me to know myself, what motivates me, who my support system is, and self-knowledge. That allows me to see my sense of life and, therefore, my sense of purpose. CSLM has helped me find my sense of transcendence and how the results come hand in hand with serving, training, and growing. Finding what you are good at to do these last three things and thus transcend through service to others. It also helps me conduct myself ethically by doing the best I can in everything I can. I found in CSLM a model of life for me and a family model whereby we all see much more transcendent meaning in our lives."

Rafael Zúñiga, regional sales director

"I don't know where the saying 'I'm going where I look' comes from, but finding a sense of purpose has helped me set clear priorities. How you ought to be doing things, where you ought to be at a given moment, it all depends on where you're heading."

Paulina Murguía Guerrero, corporate strategy

"Having clarity in respect to sense of purpose has helped me discover that there are strategies for setting goals and creating a process to reach them. It's wonderful when you can understand that seeking your own personal growth as another goal helps you to grow more quickly."

Enrique Majos Ramírez, CEO of Gentera

"I noted that one of my young employees was out to conquer the world, but he paid no attention to how important people are. After he learned about the Comprehensive Servant Leadership Model, though, I saw radical changes in him. It helped him get in touch with his own feelings and with those of others. He has a better outlook, motivates better and is more inspirational. His staff even told me so. Becoming an inspirational leader turned him into a new person with clear ideas and objectives. He zeroed in on his sense of purpose, and everything changed."

Mario Alberto Gómez, regional sales director

External Dimension. Component No. 7

Serving Others
Humility, charity, and solidarity

This is a core component of the Comprehensive Servant Leadership Model, because serving others shows genuine interest in their wellbeing. When we interact with others and constantly put our talents and capacities at their disposal of our own free will, we are paving the path to happiness.

Servant Leadership gives us the opportunity to experience a sense of joy and fulfillment that comes from the bottom of the heart. Serving others means discovering the beauty of unconditional love, because serving others is a question of love, and he who doesn't live to serve is of no service to life. Period.

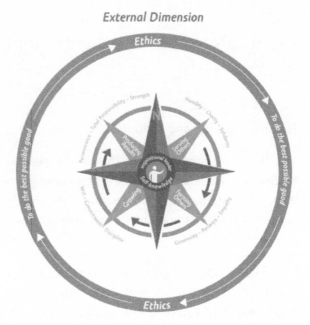

The Japanese warriors of old went by the name "samurai", which literally means "those who serve". In our experience, the virtues of humility, charity and solidarity are a prerequisite to integrating this component of the CSLM into our lives.

Beyond a doubt, serving others is one of the most important commitments and skills of an inspirational leader. Dear reader, it is time to ask yourself if you have the vocation to serve or not, because serving others requires generosity, solidarity and a hefty dose of humility. Only by serving others can we form them, grow and produce results.

Serving means thinking about others before ourselves. It demands a sense of purpose larger than ourselves, something that overshadows our ego and personal plans. Serving those around us the way they want and need to be served requires taking the time to get to know them and becoming privy to their dreams.

> Sitting down, Jesus called the Twelve and said: "Anyone who wants to be first must be the very last and the servant of all."
>
> The Gospel According to St. Mark, ch. 9

Serving others demands giving the best of ourselves: our time, listening, our prayers. Serving others is at once a great privilege and a huge responsibility. It is, without a doubt, the lifestyle the inspirational leader chooses, because in the final reckoning, what we have done for God and our fellow men is all that will count.

If you're reading this book, the chances are you're someone who wants to make a difference in the world and become an inspirational leader. Congratulations for taking the time to do it. All it takes is a willingness to commit to serving others and to be part of the transformation.

Bring about the transformation you'd like to see in others in yourself by serving them as Jesus Christ and Saint Teresa taught us.

The more we give to others, the fuller and more rewarding our lives will be. This is the key to putting Servant Leadership into action and becoming a leader who inspires those around you with your example. In short: if you aren't burning with love, a lot of people are going to die of cold.

There is a passage from the Bible that says: "I am the good shepherd; the good shepherd lays down his life for the sheep. The hired hand is not the shepherd and does not own the sheep. So when he sees the wolf coming, he abandons the sheep and runs away. Then the wolf attacks the flock and scatters it. The man runs away because he is a hired hand and cares nothing for the sheep. I am the good shepherd; I know my sheep and my sheep know me." (John 10, 11-18)

Some examples of serving:
Showing sincere interest in the personal and professional lives of others (subordinates, superiors and peers)
Sincerely offering to help out on altruistic projects
Respecting others' dignity
Anticipating the needs of others and sincerely trying to help them satisfy them

Dr. Jerrilou Johnson Herman[19] says: "We should treat others the way they need and want to be treated." Jesus himself taught us that loving is giving. In other words, the more you give, the more you love, and no love is greater than being willing to give your life for a friend.

When we devote our lives to serving others; when we live to give and not to take; when we're willing to suffer so others can be happy, then we can say we are disciples of the Lord.

Every day we need to sow something, regardless of whether or not we get to see the fruits. This is not up to us. Our duty is to serve. It is God who decides how, when, where and to whom the fruits of our labor will go.

---

[19] Psychotherapist certified as an executive coach, conflict mediator and group counselor. A creator of corporate education programs, she is recognized for her work on Servant Leadership and on transforming individuals, work teams and their organizations. She is a graduate of the UNAM and teaches at the Instituto Tecnológico Autónomo de México (ITAM).

> "At the end of life, like after a game of chess, the king and the pawn go into the same box."
>
> Italian proverb

This reminds me of Jorge Bucay's story about old Eliahu, who was kneeling beside some date palms in a remote desert oasis when his neighbor, the wealthy merchant Hakim, stopped at the oasis to water his camels. "Hello, old man. May peace be with you," said Hakim to Eliahu, who was sweating as he dug a hole in the sand.

"And you too," replied Eliahu, without looking up.

"What are you doing out here in this heat with that shovel?" asked Hakim.

"Sowing," replied Eliahu.

"What are you sowing here, Eliahu?"

"Dates," replied the old man and pointed at the palm grove around him.

"Dates!!" said Hakim and rolled his eyes as if he'd just heard the stupidest thing. "Dear friend, the heat has gone to your head. Put that shovel down, and let's go to the tent and have a drink.

"I can't. I have to finish planting. We can drink later if you want..."

"Tell me, my friend, how old are you?"

"I don't know. 60, 70, 80. I forget, but what does it matter?"

"Listen, my friend, it takes date palms over 50 years to grow, and only when they've matured do they bear fruit. You know I wish you no ill. I hope you live to 101, but you know it's not likely you'll get to harvest what you have sown today. Put that shovel down, and come with me."

"Listen, Hakim, I've eaten dates others have sown; others who never expected to taste them. Today I am sowing so another can eat the dates I have planted today, and even if it is only in honor of that stranger, it's worth completing my task."

"You've taught me a valuable lesson, Eliahu. Let me give you a bag of coins in return for the wisdom you have shared with me today," and with that, Hakim put a leather bag in the old man's hand.

"Thank you for your coins, my friend. Sometimes it happens: you predicted I wouldn't get to reap what I had sowed, and it seemed you were right, but look! I haven't even finished sowing and I've already harvested a bag of coins and the gratitude of a friend."

To conclude, serving others requires, first and foremost, humility. There are things you must know and do to be an inspirational leader, but the most important one is to live in the here and now.

"Whether we want to be or not, we're all inspirational leaders of a sort. It's a matter of seeking to be good, of being aware that we should do good deeds. With this in mind, we become totally different."

Enrique Majos Ramírez, CEO of Gentera

"Throughout my life, I've always been convinced that the service factor leads to transcendence, so the idea of Servant Leadership that came up in the leadership programs was enough for me to leave family, home, friends and hometown to join the dream. I feel blessed for having participated in building a new prototype: 'The truly inspirational leader is he who serves others.' Serving is loving, and it engenders fulfillment, always seeking others' wellbeing. My experiences in the leadership programs have shown me that serving is a means for transformation, for transcendence, as well

as a chance to make your mark so that others can also serve. Here I realized that God gives us happiness in the guise of service to others. Here it dawns on me that service is not a matter of religion but rather has to do with leading in the most powerful way possible toward a better world. Here I happily discover that in serving, the soul expands and propels us into a virtuous circle of service, with the profound conviction that serving is not a means but rather an end in itself. A sublime end that takes us beyond and fosters living with meaning throughout our lifetime."

Hugo Cantú, leadership

"The Comprehensive Servant Leadership Model poses meaningful questions to us. In going over each of the model's facets, you inevitably ask yourself a thousand questions. Am I serving because it's my job or am I exercising generosity? Am I serving because I'm exercising generosity in seeking the other's welfare?"

Horacio D'argence González, leadership

External Dimension. Component No. 8
Forming Others

Generosity, patience, and empathy

Once upon a time, in a small town near Edgerton, Wisconsin, there was farmer who had seven daughters. The man would go into town every da and organize sporting activities for the local boys. For years, he would tal to them and give them advice, until the boys became teenagers. All tha time, the boys' parents found it convenient to delegate the responsibilit of educating their sons to the farmer, while the farmer, in turn, was harshl criticized for devoting more time to the local boys than to his ow daughters.

When asked why, he said without a moment's hesitation, "I've investe all my time and done everything in my power to form those young men fo one reason and one reason alone: they are the men my daughters wi marry.

The story illustrates what genuine concern to educate others is, whethe it be passing on our skills and knowledge every chance we get or creatin the circumstances to help someone grow. As a general rule of thumb: "Th quickest way to learn is to teach and form others". To do so, you need t love them, understand them, forgive them and grow with them.

Instead of wasting our time and energy telling people what the shouldn't do, we'd do better to invest it in guiding and inspiring them. W need to lead the way and show them with our own example what to do how to do it and, most importantly, why to do it, because failing to deman the best of the people we love is indifference.

In others words, forming others is demanding the best of them, with love, because we care about them and want what's best for them. Character-formers are people who bring out the best in others and help them better themselves every day, at every opportunity; people who make sure others are better for having come into contact with them.

When we refer to forming people, the following saying illustrates the process: "If you're planning a year ahead, sow rice; if you're planning a decade ahead, plant trees; if you're planning for a lifetime, form people", because forming people implies creating mechanisms and plans for those around you, while acknowledging the joy of being able to help others align their everyday lives with their needs, desires and interests so they, too, may find fulfillment. The true character-builder has only the happiness of the other person at heart.

For the committed character-builder there are only two days in the year when it's impossible to form someone: yesterday and tomorrow. Forming others is a daily task, but it's also an attitude about life.

Forming others is a manifestation of serving and indicates that we have grown ourselves. This is where we realize just how closely interrelated each of the components in the Comprehensive Servant Leadership Model are.

> It's not about choosing the best person
>
> but rather the right person.

Based on the premise that the individual is always at the center of the process, one of the responsibilities of the inspirational leader is to form others, but at this point you might be asking yourself: How? Where? When? Who should I educate? To answer these questions, we need to begin by understanding that forming others is a vocation, one that requires a generous and selfless commitment.

Another way to look at it is that forming others is showing Christian charity, a task that cannot and may not be delegated. It is a personal undertaking, a lifestyle that requires being convinced we have a mission to fulfill, a priority in our lives and a wonderful opportunity to leave our mark on the world.

Seen in this light, the opportunities to form others are endless: every e-mail, every phone call, every meeting, every trip, every minute of every day. All we need to do is make ourselves available.

As for who to focus our energies on, it's not about choosing the best person but rather the right person. Remember, to form others we need to be able to listen, observe, be patient and sacrifice ourselves. Our own life testimony can change lives, too, but it will only be credible if our thoughts, words and actions are consistent and provided we always act ethically, i.e. in the interests of the greatest good.

Forming others requires sharing our experience and who we are, praying for the people whose lives we have touched and being available for them at all times. It is a task we can't put off until we have some time to spare or for when we feel like it; we have to be there for others when they need us, which isn't always at a convenient time, but therein is the real test, the moment of truth.

To sum up, forming others is about guiding, teaching, and sharing knowledge and experiences, side by side. No one else is going to do it for us, so why light a lantern only to hide it under a table?

The Sermon on the Mount narrates the miracle Jesus performed when he fed 5,000 people with five loaves of bread and two fish and still had enough left over to fill 12 baskets.

We only have five loaves of bread and two fish. Obviously we're limited in what we can do, but if we place everything we have in Christ's hands, if we trust in Him more than we trust in ourselves, then we can be sure we will make a difference for the good of his Kingdom, in our hearts and in society.

We need to offer up to Jesus everything we are and everything we possess; put our five loaves of bread and two fish in his hands and trust He will work through us and help us become leaders who live to serve and inspire others. We need to follow his example. Jesus willingly gave his life for his people, just as He would for us today. He knew his people, just as He knows us. He always knew what others needed, just as He knows what we need. And He always took the initiative to get close to people, just as He does with us today.

Let Jesus light your way. Allow him to guide you and your family. Trust that He will give you the strength to transform yourself. All you need to do is offer up your five loaves of bread and two fish every day and trust in his wise, powerful hands to turn your life into a source of light, hope and goodness.

The inspirational leader is a role model who educates with his example. A distinctive trait of such a person is the ability to get close to others with the intention of helping them and forge the bonds of trust that make feedback possible. By choosing our words carefully, backing them up with actions and taking into account the feelings our words and actions can stir in others, we can help them see where they are on track and where there is room for improvement.

The intelligent approach to forming others is to create the contexts in which they feel the desire and the need to learn of their own free will. It's not about giving others the "benefit" of your knowledge to show them up; in terms of the Comprehensive Servant Leadership Model, forming others is about sharing and accompanying them through their personal transformation.

This requires us to set aside our egos and allow others to be the center of attention by way of a formative gift.

Another important facet of forming others is related to forgiveness. It's true that the acts of forgiving and apologizing can't change the past, but they can help transform the future.

> Forgiving and apologizing can't change the past, but they can help transform the future.

Also associated with this component of the CSLM are the virtues of patience, generosity and empathy.

If we are generous enough to devote our time to others and patient enough to accompany them through their personal processes, if we are able to put ourselves in their shoes and understand where they are coming from and respect the pace at which they feel comfortable progressing, then we will encourage them to become better people and we, in turn, will be harnessing our full potential as inspirational leaders.

On the subject of generosity, I have an anecdote to share. Once a man was asked if he'd be willing to distribute one million pesos among the poor if he had it to give, to which he replied, "Yes, of course." Just to be sure, he was asked again: "If you had a plot of land and a house, would you donate them to an orphanage? Again the man replied, "Yes, of course." These answers elicited some surprise, so he was asked a third time: "If you had a bicycle, would you give it to someone else so he could cycle to work?" To which the man replied: "No, not the bicycle". "Why not the bicycle if you'd be willing to donate one million pesos, a plot of land and a house? he was asked. "The thing is... I have a bicycle," replied the man.

Forming others clearly requires what we are often most reluctant to share: our time.

To be effective, it requires unconditional, genuine love that is concerned only with the wellbeing of others. And what better way to express that love than with our actions and behaviors.

Teachers who don't devote at least 30% of their time to talking to their students one-on-one are not only wasting that 30% of their time, but the whole day, and the same goes for the inspirational leader.

122

Tips on how to help form others:
Talk to people and constantly question them about what they're doing to grow and improve themselves.
Take the time to patiently teach what you know.
Share information so others don't have to go through what you've been through.
Move away from the spotlight, to give your team the chance to grow.

There is a story that illustrates how conviction and resolution can form individuals, teams and colleagues.

Once upon a time, there was a general who was famous for his audaciousness. He was also known for his close relationship with his men and took great pains to teach and share his experience with them. In one particular battle, he and 80 of his men found themselves surrounded by an enemy force of 350. The time had come to make a critical decision: surrender or die.

The general turned to his men and said, "Today is a day that will go down in history, a day that will be remembered from this time forth and forevermore. We need to decide whether to surrender or die and I want to leave that decision up to luck." He proceeded to take a gold coin from his pocket and said, "I'll flip this coin and if it falls heads up, we will surrender, but if it falls tails up, we will summon all our strength and passion and go out there and defeat our enemies."

The atmosphere was so tense you could have cut it with a knife. All eyes were trained on the coin. The general flipped it in the air... A moment

later, it landed beside a soldier, who looked down at his foot and yelle
louder than he'd ever yelled in his life: "It fell tails up! It fell tails up! We'
defeat them!"

So the general led his 80 men into battle and defeated the 350 soldier
who had them cornered.

When it was all over, the general was summoned by his superiors t
explain how he had pulled off such a feat. He told them the story an
showed them the coin that had decided their fate. It was a curious coi
with tails on both sides.

The fact is the general never once entertained the possibility c
surrendering. He knew what his goal was and how he was going to achiev
it and in doing so, he taught his men a valuable lesson in courage an
commitment. But above all, he helped mold their character and thei
spirit.

"We at Gentera have to be aware that we're not leading projects; we'r
leading people. Understanding that is a very valuable contribution."

Carlos Danel, co-founder of Compartamo

"Years ago I had an experience that enabled me to understand what
means to form others. The occasion was what we call these day
'environmental consciousness raising,' during which we were to plan
trees in a wilderness area. The terrain was rocky, and it was really hot.
recall that none of the leaders were sitting down, and no one was givin
orders. I can picture how much they were sweating and working wit
gusto. It was a major lesson in teaching by example. Projects depend o
the quality, warmth and enthusiasm you put into them so as to inspir
people to join ranks with the Comprehensive Servant Leadership Mode
which leads to becoming inspirational leaders. And that's when it get
really interesting. We must not lose the capacity to be amazed and t
continue to amaze others."

"Everybody forms others. I see it in my children. They take in everything I do, good or bad, so I have to be aware of my behavior and act correctly, not just for my own good, but for the example it sets for others. Never forget you're setting an example."

Enrique Majos Ramírez, CEO of Gentera

"From my point of view, forming others is the most challenging part, because it requires a strong dose of generosity, giving of yourself to others and sharing experiences and lessons you've had in your lifetime with others so you can help the people you're approaching to become better every day. The best way to form others will always be by setting the example. Words are not enough."

Luis Castañeda, leadership

"After getting the opportunity to open up a new region, I remember Carlos Labarthe coming to visit, and instead of asking me about the numbers, he inquired about me, how I was doing, how my family was getting along, how I was taking the move. For me, that was a lesson, one that taught me that priority number one was, seriously, the person."

Alfredo Zamora, executive director Business

External Dimension. Component No. 9 Growth

Will, commitment and discipline

This component of the Comprehensive Servant Leadership Model is associated with the inspirational leader's commitment and "hunger" to learn and grow in every aspect of his life, so he can achieve self-realization and be in a position to give more to others.

It should be noted that we are not talking about growth for growth's sake, to satisfy the ego or meet personal goals. In CSLM terms, growth refers to the leader's constant concern with learning to give more and better things to others. Obviously, the more we grow, the better our results and the more we can give. In our definition of growth, what is important is our motivation. We must become genuine "learners".

> We only grow old when
>
> we stop learning.

We grow through learning, striving to improve every day. But let's not forget we aren't competing against others, but against ourselves. A process of constant reflection helps us decide which direction we want to grow in and keep learning. We must keep in mind the saying: "We only grow old when we stop learning."

So to grow both personally and professionally, we need to work on the virtues of will, commitment and discipline.

There's a lot of truth to the saying "No one can give what (s)he doesn't have", which means professional growth and development depend on an iron will to carry us toward the goals we have set ourselves: to learn, read, train and study, rain, hail or shine.

Substituting "I have to" for "I want to" in our vocabulary can make a world of difference. What if instead of saying "I have to go to work" we said "I *want* to go to work"? Or if instead of "I have to train my colleagues" we said "I *want* to train my colleagues."

These two verbs evoke very different feelings. Moreover, "I have to" victimizes us, while "I want to" empowers us.

This, however, requires making a commitment to oneself and to others that is strong enough to lend our efforts and sacrifices meaning. Having a "what for" is of enormous help when it comes to sustaining a personal growth commitment.

Finally, being disciplined means being organized, punctual and orderly, which, in turn, will make it easier for us to reach our goals.

If we are committed to growing and improving ourselves on a daily basis, those around us will reap benefits, too, especially our families, friends and loved ones.

We are all meant to become the best possible version of ourselves, so we can honor God with our lives. Let's not forget we are God's helpers and that to fulfill this task to the letter we need to grow in all areas of our lives, in every FISSEP dimension. We need to lead balanced, well-rounded lives, with a growth plan that encourages us to keep aspiring to be inspirational leaders.

The goal is to evolve from a state of unconscious incompetence to one of conscious incompetence, then to conscious competence and, finally unconscious competence, at which point we do things well and concentrate fully without even thinking about it. The challenge then becomes to keep on improving. This process is related to fulfillment, which Mihály Csikszentmihályi[20] describes as a state of flow. To achieve such a state, we need:

1. Clear goals (expectations and norms are clear-cut and goals are attainable given the person's skill set).

2. Focus and concentration (a person dealing with a single task will be able to focus and delve into it).

3. Immediate and unambiguous feedback (successes and failures become obvious as the activity progresses, and the person's behavior can be adjusted accordingly).

4. Skill-challenge balance (the activity should neither be too easy nor too difficult).

5. The activity is intrinsically rewarding and thus appears effortless.

To sum up, a state of flow is one in which body and mind work harmoniously (fluidly and effortlessly) as one while performing an activity that makes the person feel fulfilled.

To the extent that we grow and develop our skills, accumulate experience and gain awareness, our performance improves. It's like learning to walk or run. With practice, we can do it and do it well without even thinking. Similarly, we will eventually become unconsciously competent inspirational leaders. This is the last peak to be climbed.

---

[20] Mihály Csikszentmihályi (1934) is professor of psychology at Claremont Graduate University, in California. He was chairman of the psychology department at the University of Chicago and the sociology and anthropology department at Lake Forest University. He is renowned for his work on the subject of happiness, creativity, subjective wellbeing and fun, but he is most famous for coming up with the idea of flow, a subject to which he has devoted many years. He is the author of several books and over 120 articles on psychology.

> Growing means being open
> to change.

In addition to a personal growth plan, it's a good idea to make a list of our experiences so we can analyze and understand them, learn from them and share them with others. This will help us broaden our horizons and encourage us to experiment with activities that foster growth, like travel, pastimes and meeting new people.

This list will give us a very special, unique perspective.

Before we can give to others, first we need to be at peace with ourselves, and one prerequisite to this is to stay on an upward growth path. It doesn't matter if we take giant or baby steps, as long as we are committed to constantly expanding our minds and spirits.

Growing means being open to change, so we can pass on more and better things to those around us. It means learning to learn and developing the curiosity to investigate and try things we might otherwise not have experienced. It's never too late to become a better human being. "People don't change" is another paradigm we need to leave behind us.

There is one golden rule, however, and that is that our thoughts determine who we become. In this sense, growing means appreciating and using feedback as a tool for growth, because it offers us a window on ourselves, revealing things about us we may not otherwise have realized. It's about being willing to open the floodgates and make our lives open books, while trusting that the process, although it makes us vulnerable, will be equally enriching and helpful for both parties.

If you look at our model, you'll see that will, commitment and discipline are closely associated with growth. These are virtues we need to work on perfecting our whole lives.

If we make these virtues part of our lives, we will no doubt be in a better position to further our growth. Remember, no one else can assume responsibility for our personal development, which is why it is so

129

important we muster the will to work on this aspect of our lives with dedication and discipline.

The real leaders of the future are clearly those people who are able to learn from their experiences and stay open to new ideas. For growth to be effective, we have to make it a goal in our lives, tackle it with intent and follow up with constant self-examination.

We should set ourselves goals not just to achieve them but as challenge to be enjoyed, because if we don't keep raising the bar we won't grow.

Over the years, I have made a conscious effort not to judge, control or blame people. I have tried to be flexible and share my knowledge and experiences with others. I have also been willing to make the necessary changes in the interests of my happiness and this has had a tangible impact on my life and been a transformational force.

Some examples of growth:
Always assume a humble attitude, so you can learn from every situation. Remember, learning is a constant possibility.
Keep a spirit of adventure alive, so you have the curiosity to take courses and attend personal development talks.
Be aware of your weaknesses, accept them, inform others of them and work on them with a view to improving your relationships at home and in the workplace.
Experience new things that help identify potential ideas, projects or talents that may be useful for making yourself and the people around you better.
Be open to giving and receiving feedback, and be

> willing to change when you learn something new about yourself. Make sure you balance out negative comments with positive ones.

> Finally, bear in mind the words of Jerrilou Johnson: "Ever-green, ever-growing", i.e. always open to learning experiences that blossom into self-fulfillment.

"For me, growing is an exercise in humility because it means seeking to be better, which you cannot do if you don't have the humility to recognize that you are imperfect and to accept and appreciate the opportunity that only humans have to reinvent themselves every day and give others the best that's in them. I can say that one of my biggest lessons is that, in order to grow, you have to have backbone because it takes a lot of effort and letting go of whatever stands in our way of becoming better."

Dulce Molina, leadership

"The Comprehensive Servant Leadership Model helps each person differently, but it ends up being tailor-made for each person to grow to the degree he or she wants."

Enrique Majos Ramírez, CEO of Gentera

"I've seen a lot of people mature at Gentera. I've seen folks who just work, work, work. When they examine their life, though, they find out that's OK, but it's not the comprehensive and inspirational leadership of Gentera."

Ayleen Cortés, philosophy, and social vocation director

"No matter what happens to you, illness, a divorce, what have you, it's the attitude with which you face it that's important. In my own case, at 52 years of age I had to face up to having diabetes and a marriage coming to an end after 27 years. At first I thought it was all over for me, I felt immense loneliness. But thanks to Compartamos and to getting back in touch with God and having the willpower to not give up, I was able to keep growing in

131

every area. Now I'm happy with my job and have remarried, and I'm really appreciative of the people who helped me come back from the most critical situation I've ever been in."

José Luis Núñez, leadership

External Dimension. Component No. 10
Producing Results

Perseverance, total responsibility and strength

This component refers to our ability to accomplish the goals we set ourselves efficiently and responsibly, driven by the healthy ambition to "do more with less" in order to guarantee we produce results and meet our commitment to serve and form others and to grow.

To recap, the premise is that we are geared to produce results, but that doesn't mean we should sacrifice the other commitments we have undertaken in the process. It's about working for others, for that other person, to make the intangible tangible.

Producing results without serving, growing or forming others isn't sustainable in the long term and is tantamount to putting the cart before the horse.

The first question I ask myself when it comes to producing results is, "What for?" And I tell myself: "At the end of my life, when I am standing in front of God, I hope to be totally bereft of the gifts He gave me so I can say 'I invested every last drop of what you gave me in my own growth and that of those who shared my life.'"

> "It is not the strongest of the species that survives, nor the most intelligent, but the one most responsive to change".
>
> Charles Darwin

In short, whoever serves, forms and grows will invariably produce consistent, long-lasting results, the kind of results we're used to seeing at Gentera.

But to produce results, first we have to be clear as to the "what for?" Someone who has something to live for can tolerate the "how", no matter what form it takes, if it means realizing his or her dream. Other important questions to ask are: what makes these particular results worthwhile? What impact or benefit will they have for me or others?

If you are clear as to the answers, you're already halfway to achieving the results you're after. The other 50% will depend on our actions, how well organized we are, how responsible we are and our capacity to inspire others.

Not long ago, I read an article by Lou Tice in which he discusses the difference between mediocrity and greatness. Truth be told, they're not as far apart as we might think. Let me explain: in professional baseball, for example, most batters hit 25% of the balls they're thrown, which means they hit one out of every four or two out of every ten. When a player can hit three out of ten, he is deemed a star and is inducted into the Hall of Fame. In other words, it only takes one hit to set a successful player apart from an average one.

So what would be the difference between a successful manager and a run-of-the-mill one? Between a successful co-worker and an ordinary one? Or between an inspirational leader and an ordinary leader or boss? What is that one hit that differentiates someone who is inspirational and someone who is not?

If we want to produce results, we need to start focusing more on what we want and less on what we're afraid of. Our untapped potential will only reveal itself when we venture out of our comfort zone and find ourselves in unfamiliar territory. How can we know what we're capable of if we don't try, if we don't take risks, if we don't leave our comfort zone? Anything's possible, but to make it happen, we have to attempt the impossible, over and over again. Producing results requires assuming responsibility, or better put, "respons-ability", which is the ability to respond, and avoid the trap of "culp-ability" or the ability to assign blame.

In other words, true freedom only comes with responsibility. An inspirational leader commits himself to producing results, while growing, serving and forming others in the process. The one goes hand-in-hand with the other.

We humans were created to reach for our ideals and be successful, and to the extent that we accomplish our goals, we feel useful and fulfilled. This is our calling. It also means that producing results is more of a means than an end in and of itself. At this point, I would like to underscore the role of cooperation. It is our responsibility to smash paradigms and foster authentic cooperation with the competition, because this is a highly effective means of producing results. It is –or should be– a personal duty to ask ourselves every day if what we are doing today is going to take us to the place we want to be tomorrow. This implies adopting a culture that not only allows but encourages us to measure our contribution, be it in numbers or something less tangible, which, in turn, requires infrastructure that enables us to gauge our progress and compare the goals we have set ourselves.

Last but by no means least, we need to learn to celebrate our victories and acknowledge results that are the fruit of honest hard work and perseverance. One way of celebrating is to pray to God and thank Him for his blessings.

By the same token, we need to recognize and reward the efforts of the people who were instrumental in helping us reach our goals. Here at Gentera, we know only too well that sometimes it takes a thousand "nos" before we get one "yes".

> So far, thousands of people have taken part in our leadership programs and had the opportunity to live and commit to Servant Leadership as a way of life.

I have said that producing results is tied in with three virtues: tota responsibility, strength and perseverance.

Producing results is about making things happen, about battling to th end with integrity, so we can forge ahead confident that we are on the righ track.

In the more than 20 years Compartamos has been around, thousands o people have taken part in our leadership programs and had the opportunit to live and commit to Servant Leadership as a way of life. These people no form a community of inspirational leaders who have established lifelon bonds and relationships and who influence communications and corporat networks. This is what we here at Compartamos call "transformation" an what we mean by producing results.

Some examples of what it means to produce results:
Reduce time delays and meet percentage targets, while treating co-workers and customers with the same genuine service approach.
Design and implement projects, exceed the expectations of those around us by participating more and creating opportunities for all team members to share enriching experiences.
Place more of planned disbursements without making excuses, in keeping with a strategy based on genuine interest and concern for the needs and aspirations of our work team.
Meet established goals.
Most importantly, fulfill our mission and remain true to our sense of purpose.

They say life is like a race, that it is won on the uphill stretches, and this might just be true. In the words of Gentera president Carlos Labarthe: "Make things happen, and if you aren't good, get good." The first step is to act ethically.

"The main thing is the person and his or her happiness, comfort and satisfaction with what (s)he is doing. Results flow naturally from that.

Alfredo Zamora, executive director Business

"Although, among the factors that first come to mind is getting results, you absolutely must start off by considering the other three factors. As for me, ever since I turned to serving others, my life has changed radically. Now having a 'what for' in mind, the result flows naturally from there."

Luis Castañeda, leadership

"It's become quite clear to me that getting results is the logical outcome of having worked on the serving, forming and growing components. And the results you get are more long-term than short-term, and they are lasting and more transcendent. Getting them requires patience and perseverance, strength and particularly responsibility, because getting results not only affects you but a lot of people who may also be involved and whose lives may depend on what you do or don't do. Clearly, these results have to connect up with my sense of purpose so that they get me closer to it. If it's not like that, I'm doing something wrong. Compartamos is a concrete example of what I'm talking about. Twenty-three years ago nobody thought it would become a bank and have over two million clients, but the results were precisely due to putting into practice the virtues linked with getting results: 23 years of perseverance, fortitude and total responsibility."

Pedro Saucedo, deputy director accompanying AGD Compartamos Banco

"At Compartamos I've learned that there's no such thing as 'It can't be done' or 'I don't feel like it.' No matter what you set out to do, no matter how hard it may be, you have to give it your best shot so that things happen."

Mario Alberto Gómez, regional sales director

"Concerning results, the inspirational leader examines his conscience: 'Am I doing this job just to get results, or do I take care of the job and get results because I have values I believe in?'"

Horacio D'argence, leadership

> In this life, you decide whether
>
> you want to be part of the problem
>
> or part of the solution.

Component No. 11 Ethics

Doing the greatest good

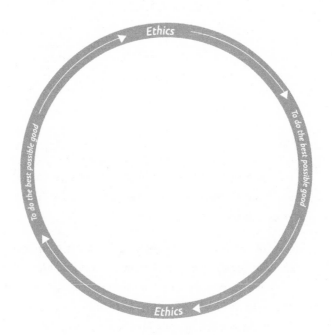

As we've already mentioned, our model takes the shape of a compass. The circle that encompasses the components of both our internal and external dimensions is ethics. A leader who knows where he is headed, is aware of his capacities and motivations, has identified his support system and takes measures to grow cannot be an inspirational leader unless his actions are governed by a code of ethics. Ethics are also something that can be learned, because in this life, you decide whether you want to be part of the problem or part of the solution.

Ethics could be defined as always doing the greatest good possible; in other words, always doing things right, not just for oneself but for others.

This sounds overly ambitious, but our goal is to form the inspirational leaders the world needs. Our invitation is to develop Servant Leadership skills while we constantly monitor that what we do is good for ourselves and for others.

> At Gentera, we have a code of ethics to help keep us within the parameters of conduct expected of us.

Evidently, the subject of ethics is a very personal one; otherwise, it could be like a car driven by three people, with the dilemma of who pays for the gas or a dent?

A rule of thumb is never to sacrifice or compromise the long term for the short term, by which I mean we shouldn't let ourselves get sidetracked by momentary pleasures or material possessions that bring us fleeting happiness or fill an emotional void but that can cost us dearly in the future or even have lifelong consequences.

An inspirational leader is someone who commits himself to the *Kia Kaha* way of life, i.e. always being strong, remaining true and loyal and not doing anything to shame God, himself or his family.

It's not just a question of doing things well or doing good but of doing everything in our power as far as our individual circumstances and possibilities permit. Remember, what we have to spare someone else is lacking.

At Gentera we have a code of ethics to help keep us within the parameters of conduct expected of us as individuals and put this heartfelt conviction into practice.

We are convinced that every decision we make, everything we do in life either brings us closer to Heaven or distances us from it, and all of us at Gentera want to make it there. This is why it is important for everyone we work with to be familiar with, understand and live our code of ethics, which can be summed up as, "Doing the greatest good possible."

This is a pretty simple, clear and complete definition of ethics, with ramifications that run deep. Doing the greatest good possible forces us to question ourselves and beckons us to "go the extra mile". An ethical person does not make do with a simple "do no evil" but does good and does it to the best of his ability, so as to benefit the greatest number of people, always putting the common good above his own interests. Sounds hard, doesn't it? And it is. It's hard to shake off our selfishness. Crazy as it sounds, to accomplish it we have to cling to our faith and allow a sense of transcendence to guide our decisions and actions.

Before he made a decision, St. Ignatius of Loyola would ask himself, "Is what I'm about to do going to bring me closer to Heaven or push me away from it?"

The question contains the answer and inspires us to act and lead ethically and thus do the greatest good possible, here and now.

Stripped to our essence, we are all upright men and women with brave hearts and iron wills. We need to ask ourselves what kind of people we have turned into with each step forward, with each new title or responsibility. Am I closer to becoming the person I want to be? Have my new circumstances, my new situation brought me closer to being the person I aspire to be or am I straying from my goal? Meditating on these questions will help you make the right decisions on your journey toward personal transformation.

It takes courage to make decisions, especially unpopular ones, but integrity is about doing what is right, not what is convenient.

We all have the power

of decision and the free will

to act ethically

and do the greatest good

possible every day.

A young man was once asked, "Are you honest?" And he replied, "Yes, of course." He was asked again, "But are you really honest?" And he answered, "Yes, I am." For the third time he was asked, "Are you totally honest all the time?" "Well, when you put it like that, no," he said.

Either you have ethics or you don't. Just as a woman can't be pregnant some of the time, we can't pick and choose when to be ethical.

In the long run, integrity and leading by example are a solid foundation for ethical conduct. This is not to say repressing your emotions is the best way to handle them. Rather, the challenge is how to express them. We need to be careful when we say what we think and even more careful how we communicate our thoughts, because a lie told a thousand times over becomes the truth.

Like it or not, and whether we are aware of it or not, every day we either come closer to Heaven or stray further from it. Every night we need to ask ourselves, "Did I come closer to Heaven today or not? We all have the power of decision and the free will to act ethically and do the greatest good possible every day.

Socrates gave us an excellent example of ethical behavior with his triple filter: truth, goodness and usefulness. For practical purposes, it boils down to: if what you want to tell me is neither true nor good nor useful to me, why would I want to hear it?

Personally, I believe this is how we should filter rumors and gossip out of our lives.

Some examples of ethical conduct:
Not accepting bribes
Not lying or covering up
Speaking the truth and acting with integrity at all times
Fostering a culture of transparency and openness
Meeting our responsibilities to the letter
Speaking highly of others
Trying to change the downward, negative, pessimistic spiral for a positive, upward, optimistic one every chance we get.

"I love the way we define ethics at Gentera: 'Doing the greatest good possible.' I think the definition helps a great deal to be clear on what ethical behavior is, because it originates or draws sustenance from what is good. Spreading the good, doing the greatest good possible, is the main thing we live for. Every time we face one of life's dilemmas, we ought to choose the option that affords us the greatest good. We make any number of decisions every day: to eat dessert or not, obey the stop sign or not, lend a hand to someone or not, pray to God or not, and so on. If we take into account which of the two options does the most good, it's much easier to figure out which one helps us to be better, which one makes me

accountable for my life and, finally, which one is more appropriate. This is why it's so important to always try to behave ethically. In my experience, we get into big trouble when we stray from the good and, conversely, life is much happier and more fulfilling when we cling to the good."

Carlos Labarthe, co-founder of Compartamos

"According to what we have advanced in the in the field of self-knowledge and how to improve our relationships with others, it is crucial to be aware that we cannot do anything without the universal values of ethics. At Compartamos, doing the best possible is the base of all relationships, and this guarantees a focus on respect for people and establishing rules of coexistence that ensure a healthy work environment. Ethics is the basis of all our actions and decisions, even if it sometimes represents more investment or expense."

Mauricio García, portfolio management director

"If you have a doubt, go back to ethics, to the question 'How can we do the greatest good possible?' That's how we can become better individuals, better children, better parents, better colleagues and so on. You can offer anything. That's how you figure out you're going to become better. You can't lose."

Mario Alberto Gómez, regional sales director

"The matter of ethics is crucial. If it's not clear to you, you run the risk of getting sidetracked any time. We can live totally according to the model, but if you don't frame it in a code of ethics, you're in danger of doing unethical things, and that's a lost cause."

Horacio D'argence González, leadership

Harvard University's course on happiness has lifted the spirits of thousands. I have borrowed some tips and simple techniques from it that I have found to be effective at making us happier and keeping us that way.

Tip No. 1. Get exercise. Walk, go to the gym, practice yoga, swim, anything that gets you up and about. According to the experts, 30 minutes of exercise a day is more effective than any antidepressant at fighting off sadness and stress.

Tip No. 2. Eat breakfast. Some people skip the first meal of the day because they don't have time for it or they think they'll put on weight if they have it. Serious studies, however, have revealed that people who eat breakfast have higher energy levels and are able to think more clearly and perform their tasks more efficiently.

Tip No. 3. Be grateful for what you have. Make a list of ten things in your life that bring you happiness. Making a gratitude list forces us to focus on good things.

Tip No. 4. Be assertive. Ask for what you want, and speak your mind. It's a proven fact that being assertive helps boost self-esteem, while suffering in silence leads to sadness and frustration.

Tip No. 5. Invest in experiences, not material possessions. The vast majority of people –75%– feel happier when they spend their money on trips, courses and classes, while only the remaining 25% is happier buying things.

Tip No. 6. Face your challenges head on. Don't put off until tomorrow what you can do today. Studies have shown that the more we put something off, the more anxious and stressed we become. Make a manageable list of weekly tasks, and carry them out.

Tip No. 7. Stick photos of your loved ones, attractive souvenirs and motivational phrases on your refrigerator, computer, desk, bedroom...

Literally fill your life with happy memories.

Tip No. 8. Always greet people, and be kind to others. Over 100 studies have confirmed that smiling alone can change moods.

Tip No. 9. Wear comfortable shoes. According to Dr. Keith Wapner, former president of the American Orthopaedic Foot and Ankle Society, "If your feet hurt, it makes you irritable."

Tip No. 10. Be aware of your posture. Walking with your shoulders pulled slightly back and your head held high helps to stay in a good mood.

Tip No. 11. Listen to music. It's a fact that hearing music makes people want to sing and dance, making life more joyful.

Tip No. 12. Food affects mood. Eating something light every three or four hours helps keep blood sugar levels stable. Don't skip meals, and avoid processed foods with white flour and sugar. A varied diet works best for most of us.

Tip No. 13. Take care of your appearance. 41% of people say they feel happier when they feel good about how they look. Don't look or be messy.

Tip No. 14. Enjoy what you do. It's not doing what we want that makes us happy, but enjoying what we do.

Tip No. 15. Don't lose touch with God. Being religious isn't the same as being spiritual. Don't lose sight of your divine origin, and stay tuned to that energy. All you have to do is connect with God and let Him guide your actions.

CSLM Work Sheets

Below you will find some work sheets to get you started on your personal Servant Leadership plan. Once you know your motivations and are familiar with each component of the model, you will be ready to set out on this journey of self-discovery and self-betterment. Your face is at the center of this plan to remind you there is no one else like you in the world and that your personal development depends on you alone.

Internal Dimension

✦ **1. Sense of purpose** (create a note on your e-reader)

✦ Where are you headed? (Create a note on your e-reader)

✦ What for? (Create a note on your e-reader)

✦ **2. Motivation** (create a note on your e-reader)

✦ What inspires you? (Create a note on your e-reader)

✦ **3. Values** (create a note on your e-reader)

✦ What guides you? (Create a note on your e-reader)

✦ **4. Support system** (create a note on your e-reader)

✦ Who is in your support system? (Create a note on your e-reader)

✦ **5. Capacities** (create a note on your e-reader)

✦ What are you good at? (Create a note on your e-reader)

✦ **6. FISSEP** (create a note on your e-reader)

✦ Are you leading a well-rounded life? (Create a note on your e-reader)

External dimension

- **7. Serving** (create a note on your e-reader)
- Humility (create a note on your e-reader)
- Charity (create a note on your e-reader)
- Solidarity (create a note on your e-reader)

- **8. Forming** (create a note on your e-reader)
- Generosity (create a note on your e-reader)
- Patience (create a note on your e-reader)
- Empathy (create a note on your e-reader)

- **9. Growing** (create a note on your e-reader)
  - Will (create a note on your e-reader)
  - Commitment (create a note on your e-reader)
  - Discipline (create a note on your e-reader)

- **10. Producing results** (create a note on your e-reader)
  - Perseverance (create a note on your e-reader)
  - Total responsibility (create a note on your e-reader)
  - Strength (create a note on your e-reader)

- **11. Ethic** (create a note on your e-reader)
  - Ethic (create a note on your e-reader)
  - Doing the greatest possible good (create a note on your e-reader)

A Journey in Pictures

We are each responsible for our own personal development and the course our lives take. The following photos are a living testimony to how we have progressed over the years, working shoulder to shoulder toward the same goal: doing the greatest good possible

1

2

3

5

4

1 Young university students Carlos Labarthe and Iván Mancillas, 1988. **2** Iván Mancillas and Muhammad Yunus during Iván's visit to Grameen Bank in Bangladesh, 1993. **3** Iván with Grameen Bank clients in Bangladesh, 1993. **4** Iván's encounter with Saint Teresa in Calcutta, 1993. **5** Iván during his trip to Calcutta and Bangladesh, to learn about Grameen Bank's experience, 1993.

6

7

8

9

10

6 *Reader's Digest Selecciones.* "Un banco para los pobres", 1993. **7** Jesus Christ, the role model for the inspirational leader. **8** First magazine for Compartamos clients, 1994. **9** Miguel Ángel Ortega and Iván Mancillas outside the Oaxaca offices with the first company car, 1994. **10** Miguel Ángel Ortega, Germán Merlín and Iván Mancillas during a business call on clients in Oaxaca, 1995.

11

12

13

11 Afredo Harp Helú calling on groups of clients in Oaxaca, 1995. **12** Alfredo Harp Helú calling on groups of clients in Oaxaca, 1995. **13** Carlos Labarthe and Iván Mancillas attending their first micro-finance course in Boulder, Colorado, 1995.

14 Carlos Labarthe on a visit to Las Margaritas, Chiapas, 1995. **15** First Annual Compartamos Meeting, Jurica, Querétaro, 1997: Rear; Miguel Ángel Ortega, Emmanuel Rocha, Alejandro Rocha, Eduardo Larrea, Carlos Labarthe, Francisco González, Manuel Mendoza. Front: Héctor Cerviño, Iván Mancillas, Pedro Saucedo, Federico Hernández. **16** The Compartamos management team at a soccer tournament in 2003. **17** The sales and marketing team at a leadership workshop, 2006. Mario Gómez, Alfredo Zamora, Francisco González, Alfredo Peniche, Wilmer Guevara, Luis Llanos, Enrique Majos, Horacio D'argence, Giorgio Caso and Iván Mancillas.

18 Carlos Danel, Ladislao de Hoyos, Carlos Labarthe and Francisco González on the 2004 Code of Ethics tour. **19** Carlos Danel, co-founder of Compartamos. **20** Carlos Danel, Fernando Landeros and Carlos Labarthe at the 2004 Annual Meeting. **21** Tribute to Bob Christen for ten years of micro-finance courses, Boulder, Colorado, 2005.

22 Iván Mancillas and John Hatch at an event in Morelia, 2006. **23** Carlos Labarthe and Iván Mancillas receiving the 2006 "Best Employer Award" in recognition of Compartamos being among the best work places. **24** Compartamos at the top of La Malinche Volcano, Tlaxcala, 2006. **25** José Luis Núñez, Pedro Saucedo, Carlos Labarthe, Francisco González, Iván Mancillas, Ladislao de Hoyos and Luis Castañeda, Huatulco, 2006. **26** Compartamos on the Mexican Stock Exchange, 2007.

27

28

29

30

31

27 Carlos Danel, Iván Mancillas, José Ignacio Ávalos and Carlos Labarthe, New York City, 2007. **28** Iván Mancillas with Fernando Gutiérrez at the 2007 Annual Compartamos Meeting. **29** Iván Mancillas with singer/songwriter Tony Meléndez, 2007. **30** Iván Mancillas at the opening of a Compartamos office in Veracruz, 2007. **31** The management team celebrating Compartamos' first million clients, 2008.

32

33

34

35

32 Jerrilou Johnson, 2010. **33** Miguel Ángel Ortega, Alfredo Zamora, Iván Mancillas and Horacio D'argence at the 2008 Compartamos Leaders' Meeting. **34** Leadership staff members handing over a house they built in the State of Mexico, 2010. **35** Iván Mancillas, Father Ignacio Camarena, L.C. and Chrissa Lautz, 2010.

36

37

38

39

40

36 Iván Mancillas and Joel Cryer, 2010. **37** Ladislao
de Hoyos, Iván Mancillas, Federico Hernández and
José Luis Sandoval on the Iztaccíhuatl Volcano, 2010.
38 Iván Mancillas and Rolando Rocha on
Iztaccíhuatl, 2010. **39** Taking the Leadership
Programs to the very top. Tacaná Volcano, Chiapas,
2011. **40** Participants in the Leadership Program on
the Nevado de Toluca Volcano, 2011.

41

42   43

41 Iván Mancillas, Miguel Ángel Ortega and Pedro
Saucedo with Compartamos clients from Oaxaca's
Guelaguetza Group, which has had 66 credit cycles,
2012. **42** Four generations of Compartamos clients,
Guelaguetza Group, Oaxaca, 2012. **43** Luis
Castañeda, Hugo Cantú, Horacio D'argence and Iván
Mancillas on the Nevado de Toluca Volcano 2012

159

44

45

46

47

44 Compartamos start-up collaborators with the management team at the Quo Vadis Learning Center, 2012. **45** Leadership team, 2012. **46** Iván Mancillas, Miguel Ángel Ortega and Pedro Saucedo with Compartamos start-up collaborators in Oaxaca, 2012. **47** A view of the "guard tower," where the Gente Nueva "Income-Generators" offices were located, 2012.

48 Employees who have been with Compartamos for over 13 years, 2012. **49** Good friends: Carlos Labarthe, Bob Christen, Iván Mancillas, Richard Rosenberg and Carlos Danel, 2012. **50** Iván Mancillas at the 2012 Compartamos leaders' plenary session. **51** Carlos Labarthe and Iván Mancillas being acknowledged for their 20 years with Compartamos, 2012.

52 Inspire and demand: two key elements of
inspirational leaders. **53** Iván Mancillas and the story
about ham and eggs. **54** "Thanks for being an inspiration
in my life, for allowing, through your leadership, many
people to feel important and for the dignity of being
useful and valuable to blossom in their spirit. Jesús
Francisco Pérez Zuñiga". Testimonial written at the
Pijijiapan office during the Annual Meeting, 2012.

55

56

57

58

55 The Mancillas-Lautz family labyrinth, 2012. **56** A chrysalis in the process of turning into a butterfly. **57** Saint Rita of Cascia, patroness of impossible causes. **58** God's helpers in training.

My Dream:
My Kia Kaha Family

59,60 Fourth-grader Iván Mancillas. **61** Iván Mancillas, 1986. **62** Iván Mancillas, 1988. **63** Chrissa Lautz de Mancillas, 2012. **64** My *Kia Kaha* family. **65** Héctor Mancillas and María Guadalupe Gabrielli Ortiz at their 50th wedding anniversary, 2012. **66** Iván Mancillas and his father Héctor Mancillas Rodríguez, 2011. **67** The Mancillas Gabrielli family: Héctor Mancillas Gabrielli, Héctor Mancillas Rodríguez, María Guadalupe Gabrielli Ortiz, Claudia Mancillas Gabrielli and Iván Mancillas Gabrielli, 2011.

Final Thoughts

The Comprehensive Servant Leadership Model is intended to guide and accompany us in the process of becoming inspirational leaders, who serve and form others, grow and produce results. Self-knowledge, seeking out our sense of purpose, having a solid support system, living a code of ethics and all the other CSLM components take us down the same path toward a full, rewarding life based on leading and serving others: a life of Servant Leadership.

Final Conclusions
In conclusion, our sense of purpose is what guides us. It is the north that steers our mission and path. It is our raison d'être. But to fulfill it, we must first do some soul-searching and build a solid support system.

Once we are clear on our motivations, we will be better positioned to produce results, in the understanding that these go hand-in-hand with serving and forming others, and tending to our personal growth.

The Comprehensive Servant Leadership Model is a wonderfully effective tool designed to transform us into inspirational leaders who put Servant Leadership into practice in our daily lives, produce results and inspire others — people we have not yet reached but who we now know how to reach after having studied the CSLM.

As it guides us on our journey of personal transformation, the CSLM also helps us become learners, ready and willing to learn something from every opportunity and experience life presents us.

Incorporating this model into my life has helped me learn to learn, and I have put it into practice on my travels, during expeditions, while listening to concerts and observing other

175

people's behavior. It has encouraged me to look within myself and motivated me to perform my daily activities to the best of my ability. In others words, it has taught me to live a full and rewarding life.

Thanks to the experience of having incorporated this model into my life, all I need to do is stay alert and look for the lessons each moment holds for me.

The CSLM teaches us how to inspire others and produce results, concepts that are not at odds in the mindset of the inspirational leader.

When we incorporate this model into our lives, we come to understand that we cannot inspire others unless we serve them and show compassion, meaning understanding, empathizing with and feeling affection for others, to the point where we are moved to humbly help and motivate them, always in the interests of the common good.

One personal experience in which I repeatedly felt deep compassion was playing Santa Claus every Christmas for ten years. It enabled me to tangibly and genuinely experience service and closeness to the children and find out about their desires.

The CSLM also offers us guidelines on how to develop our virtues, skills and capacities, make the most of them and put them into practice to the best of our ability, so we are better equipped to tackle the different phases in our personal development and transformation. The goal is to go from being unconsciously incompetent to competently aware and, ultimately, unconsciously competent, a state in which we spontaneously lead, serve and inspire others.

Once the CSLM becomes an inseparable part of our lives, we can naturally inspire others effectively and proficiently, without even realizing it.

Before he embarks on a project, activity, meeting or task, the inspirational leader starts by questioning his motivation and continues to do so over and over again until he has completed the task at hand. When done that way, in the end, he will find God in his answers.

For example, when we're planning something, I ask each member of the family to share his or her "what fors" with the rest of us. Afterwards, we each answer three questions: What did I learn from this? Who should I thank? And what does it commit me to? We can ask ourselves the same questions after a spontaneous experience: What did I learn? Who should I thank? What does the experience commit me to?

In my opinion, this is an excellent way of analyzing our daily experiences and gaining awareness of why we do things, which, in turn, brings us closer to our dream of being a *Kia Kaha* family.

The "what for" is equivalent to warming up and stretching before doing a sport or exercise routine. If we ask ourselves "what for" before we act, we can prevent injury and perform better. And just as we need to keep ourselves flexible, hydrated and rest up after we do exercise, so we need to reflect on what we have learned from our experiences.

Ultimately, we want reflection, analysis and mindfulness to become mental habits.

But our "what fors" can also be compared to visions. My personal definition of a vision is a convincing photograph of the future in which I visualize who will be in it, what we'll be doing, how we'll be feeling, what we'll be listening to, etc. Sometimes I can even catch a whiff of a smell, and the more details I add to the photograph, the more real and attainable it becomes.

I have named one of my "what fors" "Three Ss for my 90s". In my photograph of the future, I am 90 and am holding my wife Chrissa's hand. We are walking along the beach, watching the sun dip behind the ocean and saying the Lord's Prayer, as we do every time we can. In my vision, I am healthy, happy, fulfilled, in love and at peace.

In this case, the three Ss –which are just three of many in my life purpose– are what I'm going to need to materialize this vision. The first S is my sense of purpose. I'm going to need a reason to get out of bed when I'm 90, something that I'm passionate about and that allows me to make a difference in the world.

The second S is my support system, comprised of the family and friends who give my life meaning and whose continued support I'm going to have to cultivate. And the third is salubriousness. I'm going to have to take care of my health as of today, because this is something I can't put off.

This is just one example of what, for me, is a very powerful motivation, one that helps me make decisions that bring me closer to my vision with each passing day. Once I know what I want, it's a lot easier to identify and say "no" to the things I don't want.

To paraphrase Antoine de Saint-Exupéry: "If you want to build a boat, don't start by cutting the wood and delegating the work but by evoking a longing for the open sea. Begin, then, with the dream."

As Richard Leider says in his book *Something to Live For*, purposeful living means doing something to save this world and make it a better place while enjoying it at the same time.

Or as Fred Kofman recalls the words of Zen masters in his book *Conscious Business:* "Die before you die. So you can truly live."

At the end of life, what we have done for God and our fellow men is all that matters. So don't do anything to shame God, your family or yourself. Live a purposeful life. A *Kia Kaha* life.

178

References

Here we provide a list of books, films and links to online videos that offer information, testimonials and examples of Servant Leadership in action. All the sources listed have in some way contributed to this book.

Bibliography

——

Albom, Mitch, *Tuesdays with Morrie*. United States, Broadway, 1997.
Bartunek, John, *The Better Part: A Christ-Centered Resource for Personal Prayer*. United States, Catholic Spiritual Direction, 2011.

Bell, Rob, *Love Wins*. United States, Harper One, 2011.

Ben Shahar, Tal, *Happier*. United States, Mc Graw Hill, 2007.

Blanchard, Ken, et al., *High Five! The Magic of Working Together*. United States, William Morrow, 2000.

Blanchard, Ken and Mark Miller, *Great Leaders Grow, Becoming a Leader for Life*. United States, Berret-Khoeler Publishers Inc., 2012.

Bolman, Lee G. and Terrence E. Deal, *Leading with Soul. An Uncommon Journey of Spirit*. United States, Jossey-Bass, 2011.

Bucay, Jorge, *Llegar a la cima y seguir subiendo. El sexto camino*. Mexico, Océano, 2010.

Bucay, Jorge, *Recuentos para Demián*, Argentina, Editorial del Nuevo Extremo, 2006.

Buckingham, Marcus and Donald O. Clifton, *Now Discover Your Strengths*. United States, Free Press, 2001.

Buettner, Dan, *Blue Zone. Lessons for Living Longer from the People Who've Lived the Longest*. Mexico, National Geographic Society, 2010.

Burnison, Gary, *The Twelve Absolutes of Leadership*. United States, Mc

Graw Hill, 2012.

Carlin, John, *Playing the Enemy: Nelson Mandela and the Game that Made a Nation*. United States, The Penguin Press, 2008.

Carlson, Richard, *Don't Sweat the Small Stuff... and It's All Small Stuff. Simple ways to keep the little things from taking over your life*. United States, Hyperion, 2001.

Carnegie, Dale, *How to Win Friends and Influence People*. United States, Knopf Doubleday Publishing Group, 2010.

Carnegie, Dale, *How to Stop Worryng and Start Living*. United States, Pocket Books Nonfiction, 2004.

Castañeda Martínez, Luis, *¿Qué planes tiene para el resto de su vida?* Mexico, Editorial Panorama, 2012.

Chacón, Armando and Pablo Peña, *Cómo cambiar historias*. Mexico, Fondo de Cultura Económica, 2012.

Chandler, Steve, *Reinventing Yourself. How to Become the Person You've Always Wanted to Be*. United States, Carrer Press, 2005.

Chandler, Steve, *100 Ways to Motivate Yourself*. United States, Carrer Press, 2004.

Chinchilla, Nuria and Maruja Moragas, *Dueños de nuestro destino. Cómo conciliar la vida profesional, familiar y personal*. Spain, Ariel, 2007.

Chu, Chin-Ning, *Do Less, Achieve More: Discover the Hidden Powers of Giving In*. United States, Regan Books, 1998.

Collins, Jim, *Good to Great: Why Some Companies Make the Leap and Others Don't*. United States, Harper Business, 2001.

Connellan, Tom, *Inside the Magic Kingdom: Seven Keys to Disney's Success*. United States, Peak Performance, 1997.

Csikszentmihályi, Mihaly, *Flow: The Psychology of Optimal Experience*. United States, Harper Perennial, 1991.

Denning, Stephen, *The Leader's Guide to Storytelling*. United States, Jossey-Bass, 2005.

180

Eckhart, Tolle, *The Power of Now. A Guide to Spiritual Enlightenment.* United States, New World Library, 2004.

Estrada Inda, Lauro, *El ciclo vital de la familia.* Mexico, Debolsillo, 2007.

Frankl, Viktor E., *Man's Search for Meaning.* United States, Beacon Press, 2006.

Gardner, Howard, *Five Minds for the Future.* United States, Harvard Business Press, 2004.

George, Bill, *Authentic Leadership: Rediscovering the Secrets to Creating Lasting Value.* United States, Jossey-Bass, 2003.

George, Bill, et al., *Finding Your True North. A Personal Guide.* United States, Jossey-Bass, 2008.

George, Bill and Peter Sims. *True North: Discover Your Authentic Leadership.* United States, Jossey-Bass, 2007.

George, Bill and Doug Baker, *True North Groups.* United States, Berret-Koehler Publishers Inc., 2011.
Goldsmith, Marshall, *Learn Like a Leader.* United States, Nb, 2010.
Goleman, Daniel, *Working with Emotional Intelligence.* United States, Bantam Dell, 1998.

Goleman, Daniel, et al., *Primal Leadership: Unleashing the Power of Emotinal Intelligence.* United States, Harvard Business Publishing, 2013.

Greenleaf, Robert, *The Servant as Leader.* United States, The Greenleaf Center for Servant Leadership, 2008.

Greenleaf, Robert, *Servant Leadership: A Journey into the Nature of Legitimate Power and Greatness.* United States, Paulist Press, 2002.

Heider, John, *The Tao of Leadership: Lao-Tsu's Tao Te Ching Adapted for a New Age.* United States, Humanics Limited, 1985.

Hillenbrand, Laura, *Unbroken: A World War II Story of Survival, Resilience and Redemption.* United States, Random House, 2010.

181

Hunter, James C., *The Servant: A Simple Story about the True Essence of Leadership*. United States, Crown Business, 1999.

Jaworski, Joseph, *Synchronicity. The Inner Path of Leadership*. United States, Berret-Koehler Publishers, Inc., 2011.

Johnstone, Keith, *Impro for Storytellers*. United States, Routledge, 1999.

Jordán, Rodrigo and Marcelino Garay, *Liderazgo real. De los fundamentos a la práctica*. Chile, Pearson Educación, 2009.

Kahane, Adam, *Solving Tough Problems: An Open Way of Talking, Listening, and Creating New Realities*. United States, Berret-Koehler Publishers, Inc., 2004.

Kelly, Matthew, *The Dream Manager*. United States, Beacon Publishing, 2007.

Kelly, Matthew, *Rediscovering Catholicism*. United States, Beacon Publishing, 2002.

Kim, W. Chan and Renee Mauborgne, *Blue Ocean Strategy. How to Create Uncontested Market Space and Make Competition Irrelevant*. United States, Harvard Business School Publishing Corporation, 2005.

Kofman, Fred, *Conscious Business: How to Build Value through Values*. United States, Sounds True, 2006.

Leider, Richard and David Shapiro, *Something to Live For*. United States, Berret-Koehler Publishers, 2008.

Llano Cifuentes, Carlos, *Humildad y liderazgo. ¿Necesita el empresario ser humilde?* Mexico, Ediciones Ruz, 2007.

Lundin, Stephen C., et al., *Fish!: A Proven Way to Boost Morale and Get Results*. United States, Hyperion, 2000.

Marx, Gary, *Future Focused Leadership; Preparing Schools, Students and Communities for Tomorrow's Realities*. United States, ASCD, 2006.

Marx, Gary, *Sixteen Trends, Their Profound Impact on Our Future: Implications for Students, Education and Communities*. United States, Educational Research Service, 2006.

Maxwell, John, *Go for Gold: Inspiration to Increase Your Leadership Impact*. United States, Thomas Nelson, 2008.

Maxwell, John, *Leadership Gold: Lessons I've Learned from a Lifetime of Leading*. United States, Thomas Nelson, 2008.

Maxwell, John, *The 17 Essential Qualities of a Team Player: Becoming the Kind of Person Every Team Wants*. United States, Thomas Nelson, 2002.

McGraw, Phil C., *Family First: Your Step-by-Step Plan for Creating a Phenomenal Family*. United States, Free Press, 2004.

Michelli, Joseph A., *The Starbucks Experience: 5 Principles for Turning Ordinary into Extraordinary*. United States, McGraw Hill, 2007.

Millán, César and Melissa Jo Peltier, *Cesar's Rules: Your Way to Train a Well-Behaved Dog*. United States, Three Rivers Press, 2010.

Murray, David J. P., *Genesis: Another Chance for Parents, Teachers and Anyone Involved in Education*. United States, Circle Press, 2007.

Neuschel, Robert P., *The Servant Leader: Unleashing the Power of Your People*. Mexico, Northwestern University Press, 2005.

Ortega Trillo, Alejandro, *Vicios y virtudes, claves para un programa de vida*. Mexico, El Arca, 2011.

Pausch, Randy and Jeffrey Zaslow, *The Last Lecture*. United States, Mexico, Hyperion, 2008.

Ratzinger, Joseph (PopeBenedict XVI), *Jesus of Nazareth: From the Baptism in the Jordan to the Transfiguration*, original title: *Jesus von Nazareth*. United States, Doubleday Broadway Publishing Group / Random House, 2007.

Robinson, Ken and Lou Aronica, *The Element: How Finding Your Passion Changes Everything*. United States, Viking Penguin, 2009.

Rovira Celma, Alex and Fernando Trías de Bes, *Good Luck: Create the Conditions for Success in Life and Business*. United States, Jossey-Bass, 2004.

Ruiz, Miguel Ángel, *Los cuatro acuerdos. Un libro de la sabiduría tolteca*.
183

Mexico, Urano, 1998.

Schultz, Howard and Dori Jones Yung, *Put Your Heart into It. How Starbucks Built a Company One Cup at a Time.* United States, Hyperion, 2009.

Schwartz, David Joseph, *The Magic of Thinking Big.* United States, Prentice-Hall, Inc., 1959.

Sharma, Robin S., *Life Lessons from the Monk Who Sold His Ferrari.* United States, Harper Collins Publishers, 1999.

Sharma, Robin, *The Leader Who Had No Title. A Modern Fable on Real Success in Business and in Life.* United States, Free Press, 2010.

Sinek, Simon, *Start with Why. How Great Leaders Inspire Everyone to Take Action.* United States, Penguin Books Limited, 2011.

Swahn, Anders Lennart and Staffan Svahn, *Creativity.* United States, Author- House, 2008.

Tan, Chade-Meng, *et al.*, *Search inside Yourself.* United States, Harper Collins, 2012.

Tebow, Tim, *Through My Eyes.* United States, Harper Collins, 2011.

The Arbinger Institute, *Leadership and Self-Deception: Getting out of the Box.* United States, Berrett-Koeler Publishers, Inc., 2010.

Tice, Lou, *Smart Talk for Achieving Your Potential.* Canada, Pacific Institute Publishing, 2005.

Van Velsor, Ellen, et al., *Handbook of Leadership Development.* United States, The Center for Creative Leadership, Jossey-Bass, 2010.
Waitzkin, Josh, *The Art of Learning.* United States, FreePress, 2011.
Warren, Arnie, *Find Your Passion.* United States, Pallium Books, 2000.
Widmer, Andreas, *The Pope and the CEO: John Paul II's Leadership Lessons to a Young Swiss Guard.* United States, Emaus Road Publishing, 2011.
Zenger, John H. and Joseph R. Folkman, *The Extraordinary Leader. Turning Good Managers into Great Leaders.* United States, Mc Graw Hill, 2009.

Zenger, John H, *et al.*, *The Inspiring Leader, Unlocking the Secrets of How Extraordinary Leaders Motivate*. United States, Mc Graw Hill, 2009.

Filmography

50 First Dates, director: Peter Segal, production: Anonymous Content, Columbia Pictures Corporation, Happy Madison Productions. United States, 2004.

Angus, director: Patrick Read Johnson, production: Quality Entertainment, Atlas Entertainment, British Broadcasting Corporation (BBC), Turner Pictures (I), New Line Cinema, Syalis DA, Television Française, Tele München Fernseh Produktionsgesellschaft (TMG). United States, United Kingdom, Germany, France, 1995.

August Rush, director: Kirsten Sheridan, production: Warner Bros. Pictures, CJ Entertainment, Southpaw Entertainment (I). United States, 2007.

Batman Begins, director: Christopher Nolan, production: Warner Bros. Pictures, DC Comics, Syncopy. United States, 2005.

Braveheart, director: Randall Wallace, production: Icon Entertainment International (as Icon Productions), Ladd Company, B. H. Finance C. V. United States, 1995.

Cast Away, director: Robert Zemeckis, production: Twentieth Century Fox Film Corporation, Playtone, Image Movers. United States, 2000.

Chariots of Fire, director: Hugh Hudson, production: Enigma Productions, Allied Stars Ltd. United Kingdom, 1981.

Cinema Paradiso, director: Giuseppe Tornatore, production: Lionsgate. Italy, France, 1990.

Dead Poets Society, director: Peter Weir, production: Touchstone. United States, 1989.

Driving Miss Daisy, director: Bruce Beresford, production: The Zanuck Company, Majestic Films International. United States, 1989.

El estudiante, director: Roberto Girault, production: Halo Estudio. Mexico, 2009.

El gran milagro, director: Bruce Morris, production: Dos Corazones Films. Mexico, 2011.

Fireproof, director: Alex Kendrick, production: Affirm Films, Carmel Entertainment, Sherwood Pictures. United States, 2008.

For Greater Glory: The True Story of Cristiada, director: Dean Wright, production: New Land Films. Mexico, 2012.

Forever Strong, director: Ryan Little, production: Go Films, Picture Rock Entertainment. United States, 2008.

Gladiator, director: Ridley Scott, production: Universal Pictures, DreamWorks SKG, Scott Free Productions, Red Wagon Entertainment, Mill Film, C & L, Dawliz. United States, 2000.

Hachiko: A Dog's Story, director: Lasse Halström, production: Inferno Distribution, Scion Films, Grand Army Entertainment. United States, 2009.

Hoosiers, director: David Anspaugh, production: Hemdale Film, Carter DeHaven Production. United States, United Kingdom, 1986.

I Am Sam, director: Jessie Nelson, production: Red Fish Blue Fish Films, Avery Pix, New Line Cinema. United States, 2001.

Indiana Jones and the Kingdom of the Crystal Skull, director: Steven Spielberg, production: Paramount Pictures, Lucasfilm. United States, 2008.

Indiana Jones and the Last Crusade, director: Steven Spielberg, production: Paramount Pictures, Lucasfilm. United States, 1989.

Indiana Jones and the Temple of Doom, director: Steven Spielberg, production: Paramount Pictures, Lucasfilm. United States, 1986.

Invictus, director: Clint Eastwood, production: Malpaso Productions, Mace Neufeld Productions, Warner Bros. Pictures. United States, 2009.

Jonathan Livingston Seagull, director: Hall Bartlett, production: J L S Partnership. United States, 1973.

Karol: A Man Who Became Pope, director: Giacomo Battiato, production: Taodue Film. Poland, Italy, 2005.

La última cima, director: Juan Cotelo, production: Infinito + 1. Spain, Manuel 2010.

Le huitième jour, director: Jaco Von Dormael, co-production: France-Belgium-GB; Pan Européenne Production / Homemade Films / TF1 Films Production / Working Title / D.A. Films. Belgium, France, United Kingdom, 1996.

Les choristes, director: Christophe Barratier, production: CP Medien AG, Canal+, Vega Film. France, Switzerland, Germany, 2004.

Les femmes du 6ème étage, director: Philippe Le Guay, production: Vendôme Production, Ciné Cinéma, France Télévision. France, 2010.

Letters to God, directors: David Nixon, Patrick Doughtie, production: Possibility Pictures, Mercy Creek Entertainment. United States, 2010.

Life Is Beautiful (original title: *La vita è bella)*, director: Roberto Benigni, production: Melampo Cinematografica, Cecchi Gori Group Tiger Cinematografica, Cecchi Gori Pictures. Italy, 1997.

Little House on the Prairie (television show), written by Ande Lamb,

187

production: National Broadcasting Company (NBC). United States, 1974-1983.

Lonesome Dove, television show directed by Simon Wincer, production: Motown Productions, Qintex Entertainment, Pangaea, et al. United States, 1989.

Master and Commander: The Far Side of the World, director: Peter Weir, production: Twentieth Century Fox, Universal Pictures, Miramax Films, Samuel Goldwyn Films. United States, 2003.

Men of Honor, director: George Tillman Jr., production: Fox 2000 Pictures, State Street Pictures. United States, 2000.

My Life, director: Bruce Joel Rubin, production: Capella Films, Zucker Brothers Productions, Columbia Pictures Corporation. United States, 1993.

Nacho Libre, director: Jared Hess, production: Nickelodeon Movies, Paramount Pictures, Black & White Productions. United States, 2006.

Old Yeller, director: Robert Stevenson, production: Walt Disney Productions. United States, 1957.

Open Range, director: Kevin Costner, production: Cobalt Media Group, in association with Tig Productions, Touchstone Pictures, Beacon Pictures. United States, 2003.

Patch Adams, director: Tom Shadyac, production: Blue Wolf, Bungalow 78 Productions, Farrell / Minoff. United States, 1998.

Pay It Forward, director: Mimi Leder, production: Tapestry Films Production, Warner Bros. Pictures, Bel Air Entertainment. United States, 2000.

Radio, director: Michael Tollin, production: Revolution Studios, Tollin/Robbins Productions. United States, 2003.

Remember the Titans, director: Boaz Yakin, production: Walt Disney

Pictures, Technical Black, Jerry Bruckheimer Films. United States, 2000.

Rob Bell: NOOMA (series of 24 DVDs), director: Santino Stoner, production: Dot & Cross. United States, 2007.

Rob Roy, director: Michael Canton Jones, production: United Artists, Talisman Productions. United States, United Kingdom, 1995.

Saint Rita, director: Giorgio Capitani, production: Lux Vide. Italy, 2004.
Saving Private Ryan, director: Steven Spielberg, production: DreamWorks SKG. United States, 1998.

Scent of a Woman, director: Martin Brest, production: Universal Pictures, City Light Films. United States, 1992.

Schindler's List, director: Steven Spielberg, production: Universal Pictures, Amblin Entertainment. United States, 1993.

School of Rock, director: Richard Linklater, production: Paramount Pictures, MFP Munich Film Partners GmbH & Company I. Produktions KG, Scott Rudin Productions. United States, 2003.

Secondhand Lions, director: Tim McCanlies, production: Digital Domain, Avery Pix, New Line Cinema. United States, 2003.

Shakelton, director: Charles Sturridge, production: Firstsight Films, Australian Broadcasting Corporation (ABC), A&E Television Networks, Channel 4; Television Corporation. Australia, United Kingdom, 2002.

Signs, director: M. Night Shyamalan, production: Kennedy / The Marshall Company, Touchstone Pictures, Blinding Edge Pictures. United States, 2002.

Simon Birch, director: Mark Steven Johnson, production: Caravan Pictures, Hollywood Pictures. United States, 1998.

St. Francis (original title: *Francesco)*, director: Michele Soavi, production: Taodue Film, Novafilm, MediaTrade. Italy, 2002.

Star Wars, director: George Lucas, production: Twentieth Century Fox Film Corporation, Lucasfilm. United States, 1977.

Star Wars. Return of the Jedi, director: Richard Marquand, production: Lucasfilm. United States, 1983.

Star Wars. The Empire Strikes Back, director: Irvin Kershner, production: Lucasfilm. United States, 1980.

The 5th Quarter, director: Rick Bieber, production: Fifth Quarter, Park Entertainment. United States, 2010.

The Blind Side, director: John Lee Hancock, production: Alcon Entertainment, Left Tackle Pictures, Zucker / Netter Productions. United States, 2009.

The Bucket List, director: Rob Reiner, production: Warner Bros. Pictures, Storyline Entertainment, Two Ton Films. United States, 2008.

The Butterfly Circus, director: Joshua Weigel, production: The Doorpost Film Project. United States, 2009.

The Count of Monte Cristo, director: Kevin Reynolds, production: Spyglass Entertainment, Touchstone Pictures, World 2000 Entertainment. United States, 2002.

The Edge, director: Lee Tamahori, production: Art Linson Productions. United States, 1997.

The Emperor's Club, director: Michael Hoffman, production: Sidney Kimmel Entertainment, LivePlanet, Fine Line Features, Longfellow Pictures, Beacon Communications, Horsepower Films. United States, 2002.

The Green Mile, director: Frank Darabont, production: Warner Bros. Pictures, Darkwoods Productions, Castle Rock Entertainment. United States, 1999.

The Help, director: Tate Taylor, production: DreamWorks SKG, Reliance Entertainment, Participant Media. United States, India, United Arab Emirates, 2011.

The Intouchables (original title: *Intouchables*), directors: Olivier Nakache & Eric Toledano, production: Quad Productions, Chaocorp, Gaumont, TF1 Films Production, France, 2011.

The Jack Bull, director: John Badham, production: Home Box Office (HBO), River One Films, New Crime Productions. United States, 1999.

The Karate Kid, director: Harald Zwart, production: Columbia Pictures, Overbrook Entertainment. United States, China, 2010.

The Kid, director: John Turteltaub, production: Walt Disney Pictures, Junction, Chester Films Inc. United States, 2000.

The Last of the Mohicans, director: Michael Mann, production: Morgan Creek Productions. United States, 1992.

The Last Samurai, director: Edward Zwick, production: Cruise / Wagner Productions, Radar Pictures, Warner Bros. Pictures, Bedford Falls Company. United States, 2003.

The Man in the Iron Mask, director: Randall Wallace, production: United Artists Corporation. United States and United Kingdom, 1998.

The Mighty, director: Peter Chelsom, production: Scholastic Productions Simon Fields, Miramax Films Corp., Jane Startz Productions, Chaos Productions. United States, 1998.

The Mission, director: Roland Joffé, production: Warner Bros., Goldcrest, Kingsmere, Enigma Productions. United Kingdom, 1986.

The Notebook, director: Nick Cassavetes, production: Avery Pix, New Line Cinema, Gran Vía. United States, 2004.

The Old Man and the Sea, director: Spencer Tracy, production: Warner Bros. Pictures, Leland Hayward Productions. United States, 1958.

The Patriot, director: Roland Emmerich, production: Mutual Film Company, Global Entertainment Productions GmbH & Company Medien KG, Centropolis Entertainment. Germany, United States, 2000.

The Perfect Game, director: William Dear, production: Prelude Pictures, Keslow Cameras, HighRoad Entertainment. United States, 2009.

The Power of One, director: John G. Avildsen, production: Alcor Films, Canal+, Regency Enterprises. Australia, France, United States, 1992.

The Princess Bride, director: Rob Reiner, production: Buttercup Films Ltd., The Princess Bride Ltd., Act III Communications. United States, 1987.

The Pursuit of Happyness, director: Gabriele Muccino, production: Escape Artists, Columbia Pictures Corporation, Overbrook Entertainment. United States, 2006.

The Rookie, director: John Lee Hancock, production: Walt Disney Pictures, 98 mph Productions, Gran Vía. United States, 2002.
The Shawshank Redemption, director: Frank Darabot, production: Castle Rock Entertainment. United States, 1994.

The World's Fastest Indian, director: Roger Donaldson, production: 2929 Productions, New Zealand Film Commission, New Zealand Film Production Fund. New Zealand, 2005.

To Kill a Mockingbird, director: Robert Mulligan, production: Universal International Pictures (UI), Brentwood Productions, Pakula-Mulligan. United States, 1962.

Twelve Angry Men, director: Sidney Lumet, production: Orion Nova Productions. United States, 1957.

Unbreakable, director: M. Night Shyamalan, production: Barry Mendel Productions, Touchstone Pictures, Blinding Edge Pictures. United States, 2000.

Up, directors: Peter Docter and Bob Peterson, production: Walt Disney, Pictures, Pixar Animation Studios. United States, 2009.

We Were Soldiers, director: Randall Wallace, production: Icon Entertainment International, Motion Picture Production, GmbH & Co., Erste KG, Wheelhouse Entertainment. United States, 2002.

White Squall, director: Ridley Scott, production: Scott Free Productions, Hollywood Pictures, Largo Entertainment. United States, 1996.

Videos On Line (available at Youtube)

A Peacock in the Land of Penguins

Ants Create a Lifeboat

Awesome Message from Your Son

Csíkszentmihályi, Mihály: Flow, the secret to happiness

Father and Son Story

Get Service

Great Italian Motorbike Display

Innovation and the Wheel

Joshua Bell "Stop and Hear the Music", by the *Washington Post*

Labyrinth at Chartres Cathedral:

Let's Ride Motorcycle

Los marcianitos (Little Martians)

Medieval Help Desk

About the Author

Iván Mancillas is an industrial engineer from Universidad Anáhuac; he studied for a master's degree in Neuroscience and Multiple Intelligences at Universidad Antonio de Nebrija / INESEM in Granada, Spain. He also studied Neuroscience for Business at MIT Sloan School of Management and different programs at IPADE Business School. He is a certified coach by the Center for Creative Leadership, North Carolina, USA.

He is co-founder of Compartamos Banco - Grupo Gentera, where he has held different responsibilities since 1992, among the most outstanding ones the Business Management and People Management; he has also participated in various committees and on the board of Compartamos Banco and Gentera. His main contribution has focused on leadership training through the Pyxis Programs, innovation, and implementing strategic initiatives.

During the last 30 years, he has collaborated in different high social impact ventures, mainly focused on leading the growth of Compartamos Banco, aspiring to reach the most significant number of people in the shortest time achievable, promoting dreams, and doing as much good as possible to become the Best Company FOR Mexico.

He is currently Deputy General Director of Compartamos Banco Mexico, Mentor of Instituto Irrazonable, an entrepreneurship accelerator, and General Director of Serviazgo Academy.

From 2004 to 2008, he was president of ProDesarrollo, Finanzas y Microempresa, A.C. For the last 15 years, he has been giving Serviazgo workshops to the organization's leaders and different groups of young people from all over the country. As an author, he has collaborated in outstanding publications such as *Sueños de México, Those who inspire*.

✖ @imancillas2013

◎ @imancillas15

in. Ivan Mancillas

Reviews

"I view this book as a kind of manual for happiness. What's so special about the Comprehensive Servant Leadership Model is that it is essentially intended as a tool to help people achieve happiness. It is a highly effective, powerful model that helps us enormously in our personal endeavor to become better people, a key to being happy."

Carlos Labarthe, co-founder of Compartamos

"Understanding the story of Gentera is impossible without an understanding of Servant Leadership; it is part of the institution's DNA. In *Servant Leadership As I Experience It*, Iván manages to decode that DNA and bring us a methodology that has helped thousands of inspirational leaders at Gentera grow, become better people and contribute more. The time you spend reading this book and applying its principles will be time well spent on your personal development."

Carlos Danel, co-founder of Compartamos

"Iván doesn't just tell us his own story, but that of Compartamos and its two million clients. Like everyone who has dreamed of leaving this world a better place than we found it, his voice echoes the collective voice of those of us who have seen the invisible and asked ourselves: Why not?"

Jerrilou Johnson, professor at ITAM

"Some adventurers set out to lose themselves; others to find themselves. Many set out to discover the mysterious end to their journey and others to unveil the mystery. But the author of this book is a different kind of adventurer. His mission is to introduce others to the path he discovers, taking steps to make sure it is safe and finally returning to show the rest of us the way. His journey is but a means to an end whose destination has always been self-discovery."

Francisco Arenas Ballester, professor at IPADE

197

Photo credits

 © Rectorat Cathédrale de Chartres.

For the rest of the photos © Óscar Iván Mancillas Gabrielli

___

El Serviazgo As I've Experienced was originally published in 2014 and then updated for the present edition during June 2023 for the Print On Demand editon.

Made in the USA
Las Vegas, NV
17 July 2024

92460468R00114